Issues in the Social Sciences: 9

Series Editor: Katherine Harrison

Work and Society:
Places, Spaces and Identities

Issues in the Social Sciences

Titles in the Issues in the Social Sciences series are published annually. The peer-reviewed series presents current academic research into contemporary social issues in an accessible and engaging style that is designed to immerse researchers and students alike in active debates in the Social Sciences.

Editorial Advisory Board
Eric Allison, *The Guardian*, UK
Lisa Blackman, Goldsmiths, University of London, UK
Stephen Edgell, University of Salford
Rosalind Gill, City University London, UK
Graeme Gilloch, Lancaster University, UK
Dan Goodley, University of Sheffield, UK
Jane Kilby, University of Salford, UK
Clement Macintyre, University of Adelaide, Australia
Ross McGarry, University of Liverpool, UK
Catherine McGlynn, University of Huddersfield, UK
Caroline Miles, University of Manchester, UK
Andrew Mycock, University of Huddersfield, UK
Jayne Raisborough, University of Brighton, UK
Stuart Shields, University of Manchester, UK
Jonathan Tonge, University of Liverpool, UK
Imogen Tyler, Lancaster University, UK

Work and Society:
Places, Spaces and Identities

Edited by

Paul Taylor and Paul Wagg

University of Chester Press

First published 2014
by University of Chester Press
University of Chester
Parkgate Road
Chester CH1 4BJ

Printed and bound in the UK by the
LIS Print Unit
University of Chester
Cover designed by the
LIS Graphics Team
University of Chester

The introduction and editorial material
© University of Chester, 2014
The individual chapters
© the respective authors, 2014

All Rights Reserved
No part of this publication may be reproduced, stored in a retrieval system or transmitted in any form or by any means without the prior permission of the copyright owner, other than as permitted by current UK copyright legislation or under the terms and conditions of a recognised copyright licensing scheme

A catalogue record for this book is available
from the British Library

ISBN 978-1-908258-15-1

This book is dedicated to the memory of

Professor John Borland

Visiting Professor in the Faculty of Social Science
University of Chester
2007–2014

CONTENTS

List of Illustrations	vii
Preface	viii
Acknowledgements	x
Contributors	xi

Introduction   1
Paul Taylor and Paul Wagg

Chapter One   11
Reconciling Work, Care and Social Justice:
Informal Care, Status Inclusion and Self-Empowering
Dynamics
Alessandro Pratesi

Chapter Two
The Coroner's Inquest and Visceral Reactions: 37
Considering the Impact of Self-Inflicted Deaths on
the Health and Social Care Professional
Karen Corteen, Paul Taylor and Sharon Morley

Chapter Three   73
Soldiers of 'Choice'?
Ross McGarry

Chapter Four   95
Working-Class Gambling Entrepreneurs
Carolyn Downs

Chapter Five 121
'The Buzz was Every Bit as Good as the Prize, If Not
More': A Former Career Criminal's Perspective on
Risk
Karen Corteen and Eric Allison

Chapter Six 146
Transformative Learning Experiences in 'Hard to
Reach' Young Adult Learners' Initial
Engagement in Learning
Paul Wagg

Chapter Seven 173
Work, Resilience and Disability: 'Cripping' the Norms
Katherine Runswick-Cole and Dan Goodley

Chapter Eight 196
Complexity, Capacity and Cambodia:
The Neoliberalisation of Space and Scale
Jonathon Louth

Index 219

LIST OF ILLUSTRATIONS

Chapter 6 – *Paul Wagg*
Figure 1: Triadic reciprocal causation (adapted from Bandura, 1986, p. 24).   158

Chapter 7 – *Katherine Runswick-Cole and Dan Goodley*
Figure 1: Network of resources (Runswick-Cole & Goodley, 2012).   180

PREFACE

Work and Society: Places, Spaces and Identities is the ninth publication in the *Issues in the Social Sciences* series and the second since the series' re-launch as a peer-reviewed initiative in 2013. As such, this book represents a strengthening and consolidation of the founding principle of the series to contribute cutting-edge research to a diverse readership of students, researchers, professionals and general readers alike. With contributions from authors already well established in their fields and emerging voices from a variety of disciplinary backgrounds, this book offers an important point of entry to the wealth of research that informs the current state of academic thinking about work in the Social Sciences.

While the theoretical bases and methods employed herein are many and varied, the chapters of this volume are unified by a healthy scepticism about contemporary neoliberal imperatives to construct work, unproblematically, as a source of economic stimulus, social cohesion and personal fulfillment, highlighting the many contexts in which work – even so-called 'professional' work – can be risky, traumatic, exclusive and totalising. At the same time, however, the findings presented here also reveal that the extolled senses of social responsibility, industriousness, self-actualisation and gratification promised, and yet often left unsatisfied, by formal work can be found in other areas of contemporary life usually considered to be illegitimate, irrelevant or even threatening to society.

The focus on work in this volume is a timely response to current uncertainties about how adequately traditional understandings of work can account for the landscape of unemployment, underemployment, precarious employment and alternative forms of work, which has characterised post-industrial economies since the financial crisis in the early years

Preface

of the twenty-first century. The theme of each volume in the *Issues in the Social Sciences* series is chosen initially by undergraduate students in the Department of Social and Political Science at the University of Chester as part of their taught curricula. Students' interest in thinking critically about work at a stage of their lives increasingly constructed by governments and universities as urgent preparation for entering a marketplace where paid, permanent employment is scarce while, simultaneously, often working long hours in low paid, part-time jobs in the retail and hospitality sectors is, perhaps, telling. It is to them that we offer the following chapters.

Katherine Harrison
Series Editor
April 2014

ACKNOWLEDGEMENTS

The editors would like to sincerely thank Sarah Griffiths and the University of Chester Press for their generous support and enthusiasm for this project. Thanks also go to the expert reviewers who provided encouraging reviews of the original proposal and the completed manuscript.

Many thanks are also extended to the contributing authors. It was a pleasure to work with colleagues from a range of backgrounds, all of whom, despite various other commitments, remained generous with their time and knowledge throughout the production of this book.

Final thanks go to the staff and students within the Department of Social and Political Science at the University of Chester for their help and support in bringing this project to fruition. In particular to those involved in organising the annual conference, from which many of the ideas and theorisations held between the covers of this book have emerged.

CONTRIBUTORS

Eric Allison is a former career criminal who entered the secure estate as a child, spending 16 years in prison. Eric is a determined prison campaigner and is co-author of *Strangeways 1990: A Serious Disturbance* (1995, Larkin Publications) which unveils the dire circumstances and human rights violations that led to the rooftop protest at Strangeways. Eric has also written two novels in the crime genre (*The Last Straight Face* and *Fat Blackmail,* 2009, Old Street Publishing). Since 2003, Eric has been the Prisons Correspondent for *The Guardian*. He is an investigative journalist committed to exposing unprofessional and harmful practices within state institutions, in particular sites of confinement. His profile on *The Guardian* website contains many articles, including ones aimed at highlighting miscarriages of justice. Furthermore, Eric is a Trustee for the Shannon Trust which aims to increase the literacy of prisoners whilst concurrently delivering talks to a range of audiences on matters relating to criminal justice and injustice.

Dr Karen Corteen is a Senior Lecturer in Criminology at the University of Chester, UK. Her interests are critical criminologies, victimology, the 'victimological other', and harm. Her current research focuses on the commodification of Professional Wrestlers in the USA and the subsequent industry-related harms. She co-authored an article entitled 'Dying to Entertain: The Victimization of Professional Wrestlers in the USA' in *International Perspectives in Victimology* (2012, TIVI). Karen is co-editor of *A Companion to Criminal Justice, Mental Health and Risk* (2014, Policy Press). She also has a chapter on homophobic hate crime in *Shades of Deviance* (2014, Routledge). She is co-editor of a reader in criminology entitled, *Expanding the Criminological Imagination* (2007, Willan) and she has contributed to *Criminal Justice Matters* (June 2013; March 2012).

Dr Carolyn Downs is a Lecturer in Lancaster University Management School, UK, Visiting Research Fellow at Manchester Metropolitan University, UK and the Academic Director of 'Eliemental: Breaking Down Barriers to Enterprise', a project funded by the Leonardo da Vinci stream of the Lifelong Learning Programme. She combines research into contemporary entrepreneurship education with her work on late eighteenth-century trade and the sociology of gambling. Recent publications include 'Mecca and the Birth of Commercial Bingo 1959–1970' (*Business History* 52:7, December 2010), and 'Two Fat Ladies at the Seaside: Gambling in Working-Class Holidays 1920–1970' (2012) in *Recording Leisure Lives: Holidays and Tourism in 20th Century Britain*, edited by Robert Snape and Daniel Smith (LSA Publication No. 112).

Professor Dan Goodley is based in the School of Education at the University of Sheffield, UK. His research interests rest in the area of theorising and challenging the conditions of disablism (the social, political, cultural and psycho-emotional exclusion of people with physical, sensory and/or cognitive impairments) and ableism (the contemporary ideals on which the able, autonomous, productive citizen is based). He is a Professorial Visiting Fellow, University of New South Wales, Australia and an editorial board member of *Disability & Society; Educational Action Research; Scandinavian Journal of Disability Research; Ethnographica: Journal of Culture and Disability; The Journal of Inclusive Practice in Further and Higher Education* and *Disability and the Global South*.

Contributors

Dr Jonathon Louth is a Senior Lecturer in International Politics at the University of Chester, UK. Much of his research focuses on how we think about international relations and the social sciences in general. Here, the fascination is with the 'new' sciences, such as complexity theory, and the manner in which they may impact social thought, international relations theory and international political economy. This informs his emerging work on Southeast Asia and the politics of wider economic integration across the region. He is interested in a range of intersections including links between emerging markets, contested concepts of security and critical international political economy. This has generated work on gender, everyday lives, financialisation, constructions of order and the impact of economic thought upon social structures. These interests have informed forthcoming work on the production of order, resilience, neoliberalism and governance arrangements.

Dr Ross McGarry is Lecturer in Sociology within the Department of Sociology, Social Policy and Criminology, University of Liverpool, UK. He has previously conducted research with British soldiers from the War in Iraq and is currently engaged in research on British military repatriations. He is the author and co-author of a number of edited book chapters and journal articles addressing the intersections of criminology, victimology, war and military sociology; most notably appearing in the international journals: *Crime Media Culture* (2011), the *British Journal of Criminology* (2011), the *International Journal of Human Rights* (2012) and *Armed Forces & Society* (2013; 2014). He is also co-author (with Sandra Walklate) of several forthcoming texts: *Victims: Trauma, Testimony and Justice* and *Transgressing the Borders: Criminology* *and War* both forthcoming from Routledge, and the *Palgrave Handbook on Criminology and War*.

Dr Sharon Morley is a Senior Lecturer in Criminology and Deputy Head of the Department of Social and Political Science at the University of Chester, UK. Most recently, her research and publications span the areas of violence in society, the gendered contexts of this, and the analysis of collective deviance. In addition to publications in the area of learning and teaching, Sharon is currently engaged in researching the victimisation of health and social care professionals, with a specific focus on the interaction of these professionals with legal processes. Sharon is an editor of the 2014 publication, *A Companion to Criminal Justice, Mental Health and Risk* (Policy Press), and has published book chapters and journal articles on the coronial process.

Dr Alessandro Pratesi is a Lecturer in Sociology at the University of Chester, UK. His research interests include; relationships, intimacies and families; care; care-related/assistive technologies; the sociology of emotions; qualitative methods; and social change. Among his recent research areas and publications, work on the emotional dynamics of inclusion/exclusion produced through care; the definition of the concept of the 'productivity of care' within the context of more inclusive interpretations of the family; the relationship between same-sex parenthood and anti-assimilationist forms of citizenship; the application of micro-situated and emotion-based models of social inclusion to ethnic/cultural minorities, i.e. migrant people; and the exploration of the concepts of happiness and subjective well-being in the neoliberal state. Before joining the University of Chester, Dr Pratesi worked for many years as a Researcher

Contributors

and a Lecturer in several international contexts. He developed his research interests and expertise in Italy, at the University of Florence, in France, at the École de Hautes Études en Sciences Sociales, in the UK, at Manchester Metropolitan University and in the USA, at the University of Pennsylvania.

Dr Katherine Runswick-Cole is Senior Research Fellow in Disability Studies and Psychology in the Research Institute of Health and Social Change at Manchester Metropolitan University, UK. She locates her work in the field of critical disability studies. Recent publications include: *Disabled Children's Childhood Studies: Critical Approaches in a Global Context* (2013, Palgrave MacMillan) and *Approaching Disability: Critical Issues and Perspectives* (2014, Routledge).

Dr Paul Taylor is Deputy Head of Department, Department of Social and Political Science, University of Chester, UK and concurrently a Senior Lecturer in Criminology. His research and publication interests rest broadly within the study of public service occupations and mental health and risk. Paul is the general editor of the 2014 publication *A Companion to Criminal Justice, Mental Health and Risk* (Policy Press), and has written in the areas of imprisonment, disability hate crime, the coronial process and personality disordered offenders. In addition, Paul has contributed to a funded research project on domestic violence and military veteran communities.

Dr Paul Wagg is a Programme Leader and Lecturer in Counselling Skills at the University of Chester, UK. His research interests include transformative learning, critical thinking, reflexivity, self-efficacy and inclusive learning. Recent research includes transformative learning experiences in 'hard to reach' young adult learners. Paul's writing and teaching interests include (from a consideration of the work of James Hillman) the concept of hope in the counselling relationship, and (from a consideration of the work of Wolfgang Giegerich) the interface of human and technological soul in the counselling relationship. Prior to joining the University of Chester, Paul worked as a mental health nurse in a therapeutic community for a number of years and later as a Further Education Lecturer in Counselling.

INTRODUCTION

Paul Taylor and Paul Wagg

Unlike many traditional explorations of work, this book presents a series of empirically based studies and theorisations that attempt to elicit a re-imagining of what work is, how work is undertaken, and the impact of work on those who undertake it. However, we must raise caution that understandings of the term 'work' in this edited collection are not necessarily seated in standard Fordist models of full-time permanent employment; rather the following contributions take a much less restrictive approach to conceptualising work. In doing so, the authors have overcome outmoded scholarly blockades and bastions to deconstruct the nature and definition of work in their respective areas of enquiry. Readers here are privy to a suite of critical analyses that examine work in a context of how it is socially organised, its occupying of space in a given society, and how it relates to and interacts with societies.

Traditional studies of work are synonymous with studies of labour markets, organisational functioning and employee relations. This 'standard view' of understanding work in a context of industry is slowly being left behind; indeed authors such as Watson (2012) have made deliberate shifts in their theorisations to incorporate an appreciation of the moving goalposts of enquiry, evaluation and knowledge that complement contemporary modes and forms of work. Likewise, understanding work from the perspective of routine, sustained employment and employee behaviour is somewhat anachronistic given the multiplicity of environments and contexts in which work occurs. Considering work in multiple guises and formations is no longer simply confined to radical writers, rather the study of work, occupations and society has exploded beyond traditional boundaries; something that we as editors of this book applaud.

Work and Society: Places, Spaces and Identities aims to elucidate and expose the topic of work further through its eclectic yet focused selection of content. It will equip readers with ideas beyond the conventional and almost certainly serve as a springboard to developing a critical and broadened imagination. The book brings together converging analyses drawn from the sociological, criminological, victimological and (international) political economy traditions. Insights such as these are ideal for unpicking, deconstructing and re-evaluating how and why particular phenomena occur. Challenging entrenched or myopic views of work is a principal aim here and through the use of exciting new examples, the volume gains more importance through an expansion of the critical context present in this domain of enquiry.

As can be seen throughout the chapters of this book, the nature and definition of work is malleable and is often shaped by key determinants of the society in which it exists, or the imposition of labels by those with authority who hold credence in defining it as legitimate or illegitimate. Granted, work and its multiple identities are contingent on place, space and character, and we advise readers of this book to reflect on this as they immerse themselves within the eight chapters that follow. The diversity of what constitutes work is captured here and its conceptual boundaries demystified. Indeed, understanding work outside the definitions of employment is nothing new (see for example, Horne, 1987), but at the same time, we should reflect that there is often a great deal more to know about work than has come before. This area of study will never become arid due to the wonderful ambiguity

Introduction

captured in the diversity of definitions. Moreover, those who are engaged in work – whatever its form – will always have more to say on this subject. Given a multitude of experiences, issues such as determining contexts (for example, age, class, gender, disability, culture, capitalism, economics, nation, globalisation, etc.) are an important avenue for researchers to explore and explicate. Similarly, unemployment, informal work, illegal work and household work are fundamental areas of contemporary global societies and economies that have, at times, been largely ignored. Restricting ideas of work to paid labour has been the shortfall of many reflections and explorations in the past; something that we address through this book. The area of analysis of non-standard work is one of growth, not least emanating from a firm scaffolding provided by Beck (1992) and later Castells (2001).

Taxonomies of standard and non-standard work have been used and developed for some time now, and their utility in acknowledging contractual, spatial, temporal and gender activities and relations is important. Undeniably, many of the chapters here tap into this rich vein of critical analysis and approach their enquiries and conclusions with flexibility, while preserving scholarly rigour and integrity. Increasing flexibility in the approach to understanding work and its many incarnations should not be regarded as increasing ambiguity. On the contrary, such an approach fosters a departure from codified narratives of work and its position in and relationship with society, opening up the way to more insightful and useful findings.

As Grint (2007) astutely reminds us, work is not simply a process of providing labour in return for remuneration of some kind. Interwoven in this process is the production and/or accumulation of status (which can be a positive or negative experience). Work is a vehicle through which self-potential can be recognised and a symbol of personal value. Likewise, other authors have sought to convey the interconnectedness of work with other social phenomena such as the economic context of society (Edgell, 2012) and gender relations (Cooper & Lewis, 1999; Heiskanen, 1997) whereby the behaviour of a pervading societal ideology or institution can influence the spheres in which work takes place. Moreover, at an interactional level, work can also be viewed as being embedded and having an effect on personal well-being and social relations such as family, friends and other social ties (Leon, 2005).

The following chapters begin with Alessandro Pratesi's exploration of care-giving. In this chapter Pratesi considers how the actions of caring for another can be conceived of as a form of work. Whilst care is not usually explained as an occupation or a kind of work, Pratesi argues that certain intrinsic factors involved in caring are in fact similar to those found in traditional considerations of work and can inform understandings of the complexities of caring within specific cultural and social contexts. In doing so, distinctions are made between care work and work for the market and the challenges that may be encountered for individuals and families in reconciling these differences. Moreover, Pratesi illuminates how emotional energy and 'drive' are key aspects of the caring process in addition to successful interactions between the care-giver and recipient. Here Pratesi's theorisations are grounded in data from a study of heterosexual and gay/lesbian partnered and single parent families and care-giving towards children. This study, illustrates the multifarious and complex dimensions of 'care as work' and the experiences of those engaged in it.

The theme of care as work is continued into Chapter Two. Here Karen Corteen, Paul Taylor and Sharon Morley discuss

Introduction

the potential for those in professional care/supervision roles to be victimised by aspects of their work. The focus of this chapter centres on the official state processes that follow instances of self-inflicted deaths by health and social care service users; that is the Coroner's Inquest. The participation of public service workers, for example, doctors, nurses and social workers, as witnesses in the Coroner's Inquest may well be unsettling, and as is deliberated here, potentially victimising. The study does not detract attention from family, friends and significant others of the deceased, but rather situates the potential problematic fall-out of coronial processes on individual health and social care practitioners. The authors here utilise the theoretical lens of victimology to shed new light on a research-arid area whilst, at the same time, draw the reader's attention towards not only the official processes of the state, but also other influences such as legal liability for service user deaths and the role of media reporting.

While Chapter Two focuses upon the interaction between those working on behalf of the state and official state processes, Chapter Three continues with the theme of citizens whose work represents the state by exploring the experiences of members of the British military. In this chapter Ross McGarry unearths the complex and critical aspects of the decision to join the British military. He approaches this analysis victimologically and details the impact of soldiering on those who do it. McGarry explains the centrality of risk within this particular occupation, where injury and death are very real prospects. Using data collected from a three-year empirical research project with British veterans, reasons and rationales for joining the British military are presented. Issues of social class and hierarchical structures of the military are critically evaluated in this chapter along with the responsibilities of the military to act as a responsible and capable guardian of those 'employed' in this particular 'employment'.

The subject of social class bridges Chapter Three and Chapter Four. In Chapter Four Carolyn Downs provides a comprehensive historiography of gambling as a form of work. Attention is drawn towards how gambling can be conceived of as a normalised behaviour with commensurable risks to other activities in the lives of men and women. Gambling then is argued to be a form of enterprise and as such can be considered as a source of income generation as well as labour. Regulated and unregulated gambling, the risks attached to these forms of entrepreneurialism, as well as the advancements in techniques and technologies in gambling are all discussed here. The subject of gambling, be it betting or lottery ticket purchasing, is considered in the context of social class and labour, arguing that gambling, in some cases, has provided a kind of freedom for the working class to generate income and to work autonomously.

Downs's chapter eloquently engages the reader in the topic of social class and entrepreneurial activities. Chapter Five also explores the risks of entrepreneurial methods of income generation through an analysis of career criminality. Like the chapters that precede it, Karen Corteen's and Eric Allison's contribution considers work in an alternative form. In this chapter, Allison, the Prisons Correspondent for *The Guardian* newspaper, and criminologist Corteen, reflect on offending as an alternative to legitimate employment. With experience of being a prisoner who served multiple sentences for robbery, Allison provides a testimony of why he chose to offend and re-offend in the context of providing an income. Corteen situates this testimony in the criminological literature within the spheres of risk-taking and 'edge work', unveiling

Introduction

some of the attractions of involvement in deviant and criminal enterprise and debunking the notion that crime does not 'pay'.

By way of contrast, Chapter Six deliberates over the multidimensional issues encompassing pathways to legally 'legitimate' work through education. Here Paul Wagg interrogates current education policy set against his own findings from an empirical study of students on a UK-based Prince's Trust educational programme. With a focus on the experiences of non-traditional, 'hard to reach' adult learners, this chapter considers the components of those learners' experiences, past and present, and encourages policy and professionals to adopt approaches that foster inclusive and insightful decisions when engaging with this particular group. Wagg's study insightfully critiques the prevailing neoliberal notion that education is *for* employment and troubles the emphasis on the acquisition of transferrable 'skills' for the workplace that pervades contemporary Further and Higher Education in the United Kingdom.

In a similar vein to Wagg's analysis of the social economy of work (and its antecedents), Chapter Seven considers the issue of disability – socially, culturally and politically – through a lens of resilience. Katherine Runswick-Cole and Dan Goodley articulate the contemporary social factors that are considered as the foundations of ideas of resilient identities and how those with impairments may be abstracted from or absorbed within this context, with repercussions for their ability to work and the perceptions of employers and colleagues. In this chapter, the authors deliberate upon the links with employment, social justice and disability, challenging the construction of notions of resilience based upon normative ideas. Runswick-Cole and Goodley astutely remind us here that resilience is a complex subject, yet when considering it in terms of disability, impairment and work, there are frequent opportunities for such analyses to shape popular understandings and areas of social policy.

To close the volume, and, simultaneously, to problematise the concept of work still further, Chapter Eight critiques the neoliberal world view that informs common sense understandings of the spaces in which work takes place. In this way, the book concludes with a theoretical contribution that unsettles the very ideology through which we may conceive of work. Jonathon Louth argues that neoliberal institutions, such as the International Monetary Fund, are informed by an unstated Newtonian world view, which is communicated through scientific metaphors of space, that produce notions of 'capacity' for capitalist expansion and dominate how economies (and from that societies) function. Such world views are guilty, Louth argues, of promoting a capitalist economic ontology as an ideal, final and natural form, an 'objective truth', like Newton's physics. However, the manner in which Newtonian space or spatial 'imaginaries' are conceived in neoliberal discourse is dependent upon foundational assumptions that delimit both the conceptualisation of emerging markets (such as the Cambodian case study used here), and the potential for resistance. Louth's chapter accounts for the 'schisms' or crises that occur within the global economy where a disjuncture exists between the economic orthodoxy of infinite 'capacity' for the generation of capital and the actuality of many citizens' working lives.

Taken together, the chapters in *Work and Society: Places, Spaces and Identities* constitute a substantive reconsideration of work, emphasising its unconventional, illegitimate and unrecognised manifestations and defining conditions. Each chapter is a signifier in itself of the complex phenomena that constitute work and society; a multiplicity of facets through

Introduction

which we glimpse something of the whole and begin to identify and name the systems of thinking and practice that would thwart human potential and harness it to a singular capitalist economic goal. The sociological, criminological, educational and political imaginations of the authors, challenge the reader to push their understanding beyond the habitual outmoded patterns of thinking and experiencing, and beyond dominant monetary discourse. Ultimately, the book offers an expansive vision of the perpetuation of a non-evolved, stagnated economic market system coming face to face with a postmodern global consciousness. It is this whole global market backdrop, explored by Louth in Chapter 8 and against which the other chapters and ultimately the real lives of individuals are played out, that is held aloft for the reader's scrutiny of the state of contemporary work and society.

References

Beck, U. (1992). *Risk society: Towards a new modernity*. London, United Kingdom: Sage.

Castells, M. (2001). *The rise of the network society*. Oxford, United Kingdom: Blackwell Publishing.

Cooper, C., & Lewis, S. (1999). Gender and the changing nature of work. In G. N. Powell (Ed.), *Handbook of gender and work* (pp. 37–46). London, United Kingdom: Sage.

Edgell, S. (2012). *The sociology of work: Continuity and change in paid and unpaid work*. London, United Kingdom: Sage.

Grint, K. (2007). *The sociology of work*. Cambridge, United Kingdom: Polity.

Heiskanen, T. (1997). Comparable worth as social problem solving. In L. Rantalaiho & T. Heiskanen (Eds.), *Gendered practices in working life* (pp. 174–190). New York, NY: MacMillan Press.

Horne, J. (1987). *Work and employment*. Essex, United Kingdom: Longman.

Leon, M. (2005). Welfare state regimes and the social organization of labour: Childcare arrangements and the work/family balance dilemma. In L. Pettinger, J. Parry, R. Taylor, & M. Glucksmann (Eds.), *A new sociology of work?* (pp. 204–218). Oxford, United Kingdom: Blackwell Publishing.

Watson, T. J. (2012). *Sociology, work and organization.* (6th ed.). London, United Kingdom: Routledge.

CHAPTER 1

RECONCILING WORK, CARE AND SOCIAL JUSTICE: INFORMAL CARE, STATUS INCLUSION AND SELF-EMPOWERING DYNAMICS

Alessandro Pratesi

Some of the most important and complex challenges facing contemporary society and public policy are issues around intimacy, family, and care. While in the UK and elsewhere the official everyday discourse has tended to confine 'care' either within professional social care practices or within the private sphere of interpersonal relationships, care is a fundamental component of people's lives, survival and flourishing, with significant sociological, philosophical, political and moral implications (Barnes, 2012). Care also possesses important implications in terms of social justice, equality and citizenship. Despite the fact that several scholars have highlighted such connections, and tried to conceptualise care responsibilities as a public value and universal right (Tronto, 1994; Knijn & Kremer, 1997; White & Tronto, 2004), social care policies tend to define the notion of 'citizen-carers' in neutral terms (Barnes, 2012). All this has resulted in mounting care-related inequalities, based on gender, class, race/ethnicity, age, able-bodiedness and, more recently, sexual orientation. Such inequalities become more evident in a political and economic context increasingly forcing people to manage care needs in a self-sufficient way as governments and welfare systems struggle to cope with rising costs, changing demographics and what are too often conceptualised as unsustainable care burdens.

Whilst sociological, philosophical and political debates persist, everyday constructions and social representations of care keep reproducing a collective imaginary of care characterised by myths of a better past (which was never there) and dystopian images of a deteriorating future (which, possibly, will never occur). The media and popular imagination are dominated by tales of social breakdown, of pathological and dysfunctional relationships between women and men or parents and children, producing individuals deprived of 'proper' love and care who instead may embrace the brutal intimacies of gangs, narcotics, and crime. Yet until recently, there has been a surprising lack of attention given to both the theory and experiences of care within family and non-family relationships. Moreover, both inside and outside the academic environment, family tales refer to deep-seated, prescriptive and heteronormative notions of what 'care' and 'family' should be. And yet, recent qualitative work suggests that beyond the structural changes involving family and care in contemporary Britain, the search for commitment and its moral contents are still central in people's lives (Roseneil & Budgeon, 2004; Duncan & Smith, 2006; Smart & Neale, 1999; Duncan & Phillips, 2008). The process of individualisation (Elias, 1985), if there is one, occurs within social bonds, not away from them. Rather than family ties breaking down, they appear as strong as ever, although sometimes in different forms, and such different forms also shape the different and changing experiences and meanings of care.

The meaning of 'care' cannot be taken for granted. It can have very different resonances in different cultural contexts and is frequently inflected by hierarchies of gender, race, religion and sexual orientation. Within UK and European Union social policies, for example, care is highly gendered, whereas 'work–family balance' policies tend to be framed in gender neutral terms, as it has been emphasised, among others, by Stratigaki (2004), Lewis (2006), Roth (2008) and

Kantola (2010). Moreover, while social scientists have frequently glossed care as a form of diffuse enduring solidarity (Weston, 1997; Barnes, 2012), this ignores the dynamic trajectories that care can take. The emotional tenor of a care relationship changes through time, and can encompass sentiments as diverse as affection, love, empathy, compassion, resentment, bitterness and hatred. To understand these sentiments we need to examine the full range of factors influencing the forms care relationships can take, the variations across different cultures and the difference between 'heteronormative' and 'non-normative' contexts.

The experience and interpretation of such complexity fulfil or prevent aspirations, forging new kinds of 'caring' (or uncaring) selves and 'cared-for' selves that go on to be social actors in a host of other situations. It is therefore crucial to understand the entire phenomenology of care, and the multiple factors that shape it: a major intellectual and moral development with significant interdisciplinary implications. A nuanced and in-depth understanding of what care might encompass in highly specific contexts enriches and revitalises important current debates within social sciences, but also in the field of social policy.

Public policies and political rhetoric in Western societies define the kind of families which it is possible for public services to recognise and support while excluding the others. Conversely, responsive and responsible social policies and programmes for care can only develop when we openly acknowledge and understand the contributions of all social actors, be they young or old; married, single, cohabitant or living apart together (LAT); gay or non-gay; men or women. Adding a focus on different types of caregivers is important not only theoretically, to fill the gaps, but also strategically, to increase equality. Since the discrimination based on sex, sexual orientation and marital status will most likely continue, bringing these different types of caregivers into the discourse on care and highlighting the value of diversity might be not only the most effective way to achieve more equality but also to shed light on the real meanings of care and its crucial role in people's life.

The questions then become: how do both state and citizens deal with this pluralism? To what extent do policymakers acknowledge that if we want to understand the role of care we need to empirically analyse and contextualise it in specific settings? What are the visible and less visible implications of care in different contexts? How does care intertwine private/emotional processes and public processes involving inequality, citizenship and status dimensions? How does it open new and unexplored possibilities for social change?

Emotions, Care and Inequality
Care environments are places where dynamics of inclusion and exclusion are constantly formed, often mechanically and unthinkingly. These dynamics are supported and/or hindered by the felt experience of care. In other words, emotions are key to show the grey areas connected with the concept of care and challenge conventional associations of care with ideas of burden, stress and social exclusion, which overlook the energising and empowering aspects of it. Care work may be connected with physical, emotional and psychological exhaustion but also with gratification, reward and self-empowerment. Care-givers experience both positive and negative emotional states in caring situations, and further studies on the rewarding and energising aspects of care may help us to broaden our understanding of how we can reduce the burdening aspects and increase the self-empowering ones.

Reconciling Work, Care and Social Justice

The interactional dynamics of informal care have been central to an ethic of care as developed by many care theorists in the last 30 years (Gilligan, 1982; Noddings, 1984; Tronto, 1994; Held, 2006) and several approaches to the sociology of emotions have already inspired a rich research agenda, connecting micro (interactional) and macro (structural) levels of analysis (Kemper, 1990; Barbalet, 2001; Collins, 2004). The focus in this chapter is on the role emotions play in such interactions, and more specifically on those sociological approaches to emotions according to which social structures are based upon feelings of status inclusion/exclusion in groups or coalitions and constantly reproduced into situated interaction (Collins, 2004).

This chapter builds on the findings of empirical research on informal care – defined as unpaid, non-professional care of a physical, emotional, and social nature that is provided by partners, relatives, or friends – conducted in the USA between 2005 and 2007. The aims of the research were to construct a more inclusive phenomenology of informal care (focusing on different kinds of conventional and unconventional family contexts) and to understand its multiple implications when we look at care from a different standpoint: the felt experience of care. In doing so it aimed to grasp a 360 degree phenomenology of informal care, that is, an embodied understanding of care, which could be empirically grounded and situated into specific and 'diverse' contexts. I wanted to get insights into the role of emotions in connecting 'micro-' and 'macro-' levels of analysis and to challenge conventional assumptions connected to informal care.

The phenomenological analysis presented in this chapter sheds light onto the less visible and often unexplored aspects of care. One of these aspects concerns the energising and empowering effects of care responsibilities that clearly help people not only to overcome the exhaustion connected with multi-task operations but also to balance their perceived status exclusion from other settings. Indeed, the crucial role of care in terms of status inclusion represents one of the unexpected and certainly still uncharted aspects of care. Such broader phenomenological analysis brings to the surface important and understudied elements, perhaps a blend of new and old elements, which acquire a completely new sense in light of the Interaction Ritual model (Collins, 2004) and with the inclusion of gay/lesbian and single carers.

Sample and Methods
Before starting to define the empirical and conceptual borders of 'care' and 'emotion' and their complex implications in terms of status inclusion and self-empowerment, it is necessary to say a few words about the research sample and methods. The purposive sample included 80 informal carers, 40 men and 40 women, involved in childcare or elderly care (or both). Forty-two caregivers defined themselves as gay/lesbian and 38 as heterosexual. Fifty-nine were partnered and 21 were single carers. Sixty-six carers had childcare responsibilities, nine were involved in elderly care and five both in childcare and elderly care. The discussion here presented, though, will mostly focus on some examples of gay/lesbian carers involved in childcare or critical (elderly) care. Elsewhere, other kinds of carers and implications of care are also addressed (Pratesi, 2011, 2012).

The interviewees were mostly recruited in Philadelphian urban and suburban areas, between winter 2005 and summer 2007. The sample was purposively diverse in terms of gender, sexual orientation, type of care (childcare and elderly care) and marital status, but relatively homogeneous in terms of social class. It included gay/lesbian carers not only because they have been thus far excluded from the conceptual category of 'normal' carers and from 'normal' research on informal care, but also because from an epistemological point of view they were considered a key subject to visualise the less explored rationales of care and the crucial role of emotion in determining the outcomes of care activities in terms of status inclusion/exclusion and in terms of self-empowering or self-draining dynamics.

The research was based on a multi-method approach, including semi-structured in-depth interviews, participant observation, diaries, online discussion forums between members of parents' associations, ongoing conversations with the interviewees beyond the interview context, key-informants interviews, secondary sources on informal care and parenthood collected from adoption agencies and local associations, journal and newspaper articles, and the web. All this, in order to get an empirically grounded, situated and thorough understanding of informal care, analysed in a variety of contexts. But what do we know about care from the theoretical point of view? What are its conceptual and epistemological boundaries? Defining care and delimiting its theoretical borders is the purpose of the next section.

Defining 'Care'
The literature on care is gigantic, and trying to summarise even some of its main features would be beyond the scope of this chapter. Conceptually, the notions of formal and informal care refer to the conventional distinction between professional, paid care and other forms of qualified care, and everyday unpaid care for children, older/disabled people and other adults who need assistance carried out by family members, relatives or friends. In both spheres, care work potentially includes several tasks, ranging from activity to ethics, that is,

from 'caring for' in the sense of taking charge of others' physical well-being to 'caring about' in the sense of feeling concern for others' physical and psychological well-being (Graham, 1983; Noddings, 1984; Thomas 1993; Leira, 1994; Ruddick, 1998; Kittay, 1999; Kittay & Feder, 2002). It defines a particular kind of work, an activity directed to identify and meet the needs or well-being of certain others and it challenges binary thinking opposing head with heart and rationality with emotion (Waerness, 1984). It was Kari Waerness (1984) who almost 30 years ago described the 'rationality of care' as a form of rationality that encompasses both instrumental/practical tasks and affective/emotional relations, both caring for and caring about components; a form of rationality which implies connectedness, 'local' (empirically grounded) knowledge and interpersonal relationships.

Some of the early care theorists have tended to emphasise the emotional components of informal care, some describing care as meaningful and fulfilling to many women and viewing care as a model to be extended to larger social arenas (Gilligan, 1982; Ruddick, 1998), while others have highlighted instead the material and constraining components of care work describing it as an oppressive practice to women, forced into their role of carers by a variety of ideological forces (Finch & Groves, 1983).

More recent feminist research highlights how – whilst both the conceptual and empirical boundaries between formal and informal care are dissolving – this is happening in ways that still have strong gendered impacts. Yet the theoretical dispute on the dissolving boundaries between the two kinds of care still seems to be open (Graham, 1991; Thomas, 1993; Ungerson, 1995, 1997; Himmelweit, 1999). In addition, care theorists have further complicated the theoretical boundaries of care by arguing that care activities are different from, but need to be integrated with, other activities in both the economic and political spheres (Tronto, 1994, 1987; Folbre & Nelson, 2000; Kittay & Feder, 2002; Hochschild, 2003, 2012; Hochschild & Ehrenreich, 2003; Zelizer, 2005; Barnes, 2012).

While the feminist debate on the ambivalent role of care in women's lives is still open, a growing number of care ethicists and scholars seems to agree that care cannot be envisioned as a unified theoretical category, but rather as an empirical one, to be analysed along its multiple and sometimes conflicting dimensions. According to such perspectives, examining care within specific historical and social contexts and looking for broader and empirically grounded definitions of care including affective/emotional and tangible/physical components is the most effective (if not the only) way to grasp a fuller understanding of its place and meaning in people's lives – rather than just in women's lives.

Why and How Emotions?
The examples of 'specific care contexts' (and their ways of intertwining private/emotional and public/structural processes) illustrated in this chapter are analysed in light of the interaction ritual chains theory (Collins, 2004). Collins claims that the emotional dynamics underlying the social structures (such as inequality) are based upon feeling of membership or inclusion in groups or coalitions. In other words, the basic mechanisms defining both the individuals' positions in society and their interconnection possess an emotional nature rather than a merely economic, cultural, social or political one.

The theory is based on the assumption that situated actions and interactions constitute the micro-foundation of macro-structures. Every interaction generates different status and power effects according to the characteristics of the interacting social actors and the ingredients of the interaction itself. In brief, if the interaction is successful, there will be an increase along the dimensions of status and power, if it is unsuccessful there will be a decrease. More specifically, a successful interaction produces a feeling of solidarity with a group: a sense of status membership or status inclusion, which is described in terms of Emotional Energy (EE). Collins describes the EE produced through a successful interaction as something conceptually close to the psychological notion of 'drive', but with a specific social orientation – EE is a long-lasting emotion that builds up across situations and makes individuals initiate or fail to instigate interactions, so it is simultaneously the (necessary) ingredient and the (potential) outcome of every interaction.

EE comes from various chains of interaction, and it ranges from the highest heights of enthusiasm, self-confidence and initiative – when the interaction between people is successful – to the deepest depths of apathy, depression and retreat from action – when the interaction is unsuccessful. Every successful interaction generates EE (initiative for action, enthusiasm, etc.), which becomes part of people's supply of emotional capital. It is a similar mechanism to earning money – successful transactions make people earn money and money increases their financial capital. The difference, here, is that we are dealing with 'emotions' and not money. People's choices, behaviours, and decisions regarding daily-life issues are based on their emotional outcomes and inputs; their chance to gain or lose emotional energy is strongly affected by the success of their interactions and by the supplies of EE accumulated through their ongoing chains of interactions.

Having explained the relationship of emotions with status and power dimensions and processes, we now need to describe the not-so-visible mechanisms through which unexplored and unexpected outcomes in terms of status inclusion and self-empowerment can be produced while people care for and about their beloved ones or significant others.

Care and Reflexivity: Thinking and Feeling Care
My argument is that we can look at informal care in terms of chains of interactions. I am talking here about a particular kind of interaction, i.e. the ongoing internal dialogue between the 'subject carer' and a whole network of what Norbert Wiley (1994) calls 'permanent visitors', all those generalised others who are variably present in our thoughts and with whom we are in a constant internal conversation. During their constant internal dialogue with their permanent visitors the subject carers constantly verify (or disconfirm) their status inclusion to what I called the intangible community of successful carers.

Status inclusion (or status membership) – as we have seen in Collins' theoretical model (2004) – is the indicator defining every interaction as either successful or unsuccessful, with its consequences in terms of EE increase or decrease. It is precisely the internal processes of thinking and feeling care and the ongoing process of reflexivity that make a difference in terms of experiencing care as a source of emotional drain or, instead, as a source of status inclusion and self-empowerment. I therefore hypothesise that care activity is not only about tending to or caring for someone but also (if not mostly) about status membership and emotional energy production, which I suggest are its latent or less visible purposes. Without necessarily being aware of it, all carers participate in this invisible process of EE production through their care activities. The care experience thus becomes a crucial site to observe the unceasing reproduction of emotional stratification that is the basis of social inequality and it is precisely the presence (or the absence) of care in people's life that makes a difference.

Rather than the difference – and therefore the inequality – resting on a distinction between 'different' types of carers (male or female, gay/lesbian or heterosexual, single or partnered), it becomes displaced on to a new distinction between those who do have and those who do not have care responsibilities. This argument, evidently, needs to be contextualised: it is not merely the presence of care that makes a difference in people's life, but also the presence and availability of a whole range of resources (financial resources, social/cultural/emotional capital, family/friend networks, and, above all, social services, including health and social care services). However, thus reformulated, the inequality connected to care highlights crucial and overlooked aspects of care. In fact, if the presence of care in people's lives can produce either draining or self-empowering dynamics, the total lack of care responsibilities from people's lives automatically excludes them from such possibility.

With this in mind, we can now turn to the examination of some of those less visible and unexplored aspects and implications of care. These unexplored aspects of care compel us to reframe the current discourse on care and to challenge certain assumptions, such as those describing care as a site in which gender-based dynamics of exclusion or emotionally draining experiences are often at stake. The following sections will navigate through some of these overlooked aspects of the phenomenology of care that, I claim, constitute instead its core nature.

Care as Status Inclusion and/or Status Membership
The following examples offer an embodied understanding of care, thus helping to conceptualise its complex, ambivalent

and slippery notion by empirically grounding and situating it into specific contexts. Two of the recurring themes emerging from the majority of the interview accounts are that care activities (i) connect people who would have not have interacted otherwise or (ii) make people more efficient and increase their capacities to get more things done in a more focused way. It does not matter, for our purposes, whether these unanticipated outcomes of care are planned or unintended, or whether the carers are totally aware of them. The point is that the search for the meanings of care in the entire ecology of people's lives brings to the surface important and under-studied elements. One of these elements concerns the description of care as a 'gateway' for status inclusion or as a source of self-empowerment and emotional energy production, which clearly forces us to reframe and redefine the complex interrelationships between work, care, dynamics of inclusion/exclusion and social justice.

Interestingly enough, an example of the crucial role of care in terms of status inclusion is represented by gay/lesbian parenthood. Differently from what one might think, parenthood can become for gays and lesbians "an easy way to connect with people" as one of the interviewees says. It opens the doors to the (presumed) universal language of child rearing and creates an unprecedented link between gay/lesbian and heterosexual people, facilitating a dialogue which would probably never occur otherwise. The 'connecting' and status inclusive power of care is underlined for example by Stacey, who also highlights the pedagogical aspects of sharing similar experiences, as gay/lesbian parents, with heterosexual parents:

> You have to wake up in the middle of the night and feed the kid and you have to change the diapers and you have to figure out what you're gonna do about day care or after-

school programs and all the tensions and all the issues for any family ... are the same regardless of whether the parents are opposite or same genders. And that's very, once again, it's very educational and enlightening to people, many of whom, probably, just it never occurred to them to think about before.

(Stacey)

Gay/lesbian parenthood and a family-oriented pathway can become an appealing, reassuring, and comforting option with unexpected consequences in terms of status inclusion or status membership. The following interviewee highlights an interesting contrast between a before, when, as a childless woman, she was just considered a career woman, and an after, when, as a mother, she started feeling "part of the mainstream":

having children is ... like an easy way to connect with people. And it's really ubiquitous. ... when I didn't have kids I wasn't part of the conversation. But as soon as you start to have kids – on a bus, in a training program with an executive, it doesn't matter – you can relate to so many people, you know, from this shared experience, this universally shared experience of having kids. So that is interesting, so I'm part of the mainstream [Laugh].

(Feona)

All of a sudden, the social identity of 'parent' seems to prevail over the 'sexual' identity, which previously defined these parents as gay, or lesbian. In other words, gay/lesbian parenthood redefines the conceptual categories of 'gay' and 'lesbian' in terms of social rather than sexual identities. The dynamics of status inclusion seem to be particularly evident in the following excerpt, where Kendrick, a single adoptive father, vividly and clearly describes his parenthood as a gateway towards the 'club of heterosexual parents':

> You have a different level of credibility with straight couples. ... I coached my son's baseball team, I was a baseball coach, you know. And ... I didn't come out and say I was gay or anything, I just did my job as a baseball coach. Most of the people in the urban setting are not stupid. I'm a white man with a black child, they're gonna figure out I'm probably gay. But I would have never had those relationships with those parents without a child ... And it's like you belong to their little club and you talk about the same things and you talk about struggles at school and your kid and oh, it's like being accepted into a totally different society.
>
> (Kendrick)

This aspect, which is consistent with recent research on same-sex parenthood (Clarke, 2007, 2008; Nelson, 2007; Patterson & Riskind, 2010), is certainly one of the most interesting findings emerging from this analysis: the watershed around which dynamics of status inclusion/exclusion are played is not that between 'heterosexual parents' and 'same-sex parents', but rather that between 'parents' and 'non-parents'. This, quite obviously, possesses several implications also in terms of EE production and self-empowerment. Having or not having child-care responsibilities is what mostly determines the difference between the different social actors in terms of status dimensions and emotional capital.

Critical Care and Self-Empowering Dynamics

Now, one might think that this theoretical model – care as a source of status inclusion and supply of EE with self-empowering consequences – relates mostly (if not exclusively) to childcare, and that things may change dramatically when elderly or critical care is involved. Conversely, my research findings show that such considerations also apply to elderly care and critical care. Greg (43) is a lawyer who narrated his sometimes painful but also extremely rewarding and significant care experience with his dying mother and his father affected by a curable cancer; a care experience described as a sort of 'exploration' vividly impacting on his life and changing it dramatically:

> And towards the end of my mom's life she had a lot of pain management issues and I got involved with trying to seek out alternatives for her pain management issues. ... She was in a lot of pain and I started researching a lot ... [crying]
> I: If you want, we can stop.
> R: That's all right, I'm okay. But, I went to ... [crying]
> I: I'm going to stop it here. [tape off]
> [Pause]
> R: I feel a lot, I think I feel a lot different about these issues than I would have, you know, seven years ago, if I wasn't, if I didn't go on this exploration.
>
> (Interviewer & Greg)

Part of these changes concerns Greg's choice to prioritise care over career development. After his mother's death, he describes himself as strongly determined to take care of his father and even to organise and adjust his future career choices in order to be able to do that. Although the care experience with his dying mother was not an easy path, and maybe precisely because of this, such an experience radically changed his attitudes towards career and care, and towards life priorities in general:

> And I think while my mom was sick the hardest thing was seeing her in pain. But I mean I know that if my dad's in a situation where he should be living with somebody, he's

gonna live with me, I know that and I accept that. And it's not an imposition. ... I'm absolutely committed to taking care of him ...

One of my objectives in the future isn't to accumulate wealth. ... If you're asking me about how I feel about my career and things like that, I mean I do, within the context of care giving, I feel very strongly about looking after my dad and making that happen. ...

And I have thought about career choices within the context of taking care of my dad ... I'm more likely to think about career and kind of *factor in* what his needs will be in the future.

(Greg)

Interestingly enough, the positive, energising, empowering aspects of care, or what I have called the productivity of care (Pratesi, 2011) emerge quite clearly in this quotation, where Greg highlights one of the most obvious and still least supported arguments: that is, if you want productive employees, you need to provide them with responsive and responsible care policies:

And there are some progressive employers out there that understand that there's elder care issues involved with people. ... I do job search and there are employers out there that will provide you time for elder care, that they actually have arrangements, just like some employers deal with childcare, they have arrangements with elder care. ... And they realise, you know, that in order to have a productive employee, their elder care issues have to be taken care of.

(Greg)

Critical care can activate loops of automatisms by which people just keep going and develop strategies and practices focused on the necessity to deal with the emergency, to reconcile critical care with their daily working routines; all this without losing their psychological and mental health. This is the example of Gill (39), a project manager who at the time of the interview was working for a large American company and had been caring for her dying father for more than two years. Gill's account also represents the paramount example of how care can become a source of emotional energy (EE) even in the most difficult situations. When I interviewed Gill, she had lost her father a few months earlier. However, although undeniably exhausting, care seems to become at the same time the cause of distress and its remedy; in other words, it somehow represents the source of emotional energy which helps people to keep going, even when the levels of stress can be very high:

> It was hard. I did not go on vacation for the last two years; I did not do anything but work, play some sports locally and take care of my family. And, you know, I had a drink every night when I got home, I had a glass of wine as soon as I got home because that was the only thing that I could, like I needed to decompress for a half an hour by myself. Every day was a fight, was a struggle. I got up because, and I got out of bed and I went to work because I knew that I might have to take care of my father for the rest of his natural life, however long that was. ... I got up in the morning because my dad was around. That was what I did.
>
> (Gill)

Gill's dramatic care history was further complicated by the fact that she had an idiosyncratic/problematic relationship with her mother and additional care responsibilities which involved one of her aunts (her father's sister). Gill had a younger brother and a mother who could have been more involved in the family care issues, but she was the primary caregiver. She took care of both her father and her aunt, as the principal carer. Why should she do all that? Why would she not have delegated to someone else at least part of such difficult and challenging care work and responsibility? The answer to these questions lies in what I have described as latent and/or less visible purposes of care. In the following quote, Gill vividly exemplifies a sort of enduring care for her beloved father; a form of care which does not end even after her father's death:

> He was my guy and I miss him. [Crying] I cry daily for my dad. I mean he's been gone for six months – he was the best guy in the world.
>
> (Gill)

What Gill probably missed was not only her father, but also her taking care of him – that chaotic, critical, and distressful period itself that produced so much pressure on her. What she was mourning was not only the absence of her father, but also the absence of care, the sudden emptiness created after such a dense and intense emotional period, when part of her feelings of self worth and empowerment were significantly depending on her father's need of care. Several scholars in the ethics of care tradition (Barnes, 2012; Noddings, 1984; Kittay & Feder, 2002; Kittay, Shoemaker, & Hill, 2007; Fisher & Tronto, 1990; Tronto, 1994) have suggested replacing both the concepts of care and dependency with the concept of interdependence (Dean, 2004; Weicht, 2010) which highlights aspects of mutuality and reciprocity between the subject carer and the person cared for, and problematises existing conceptualisations of the dependence-independence dichotomy informing current discourses on care in Western societies. Weicht (2010) suggests embracing dependency as both a political and interpersonal project aimed to overcome such "politically- and normatively-charged dichotomies" (p. 220). The specific case of Gill here illustrated presents us also with another opportunity, that is, the necessity to rethink both the political and experiential character and value of feminist ethics of care within the contexts of the absence of care or of the continuing care for a loved one after their death. What is missing here, from current debates on care, is the understanding that the embodied relationship with the dead person does not die with the person.

Creating the Conditions for more Caring Societies: Concluding Thoughts
Understanding 'care' and its multiple meanings and implications represents one of the most important tasks facing contemporary society and public policy today. Past and current research on care too often focuses on the gendered costs of care and on its burdening or emotionally draining aspects. Less attention is paid to 'being excluded from care' or not being socially visible or fully acknowledged as a 'legitimate' carer on the basis of one's marital status or sexual orientation. The existing research gaps on the less visible implications of care prevent a thorough understanding of the circumstances under which care can become draining, burdensome and represent a source of social exclusion or, instead, can be enriching, empowering and represent a source of social inclusion.

    The contribution presented in this chapter offers a more inclusive and thorough conceptualisation of what a notion of care might involve when analysed in highly specific and diverse care contexts, including male and female carers, married and single carers, gay/lesbian and heterosexual carers, child carers and elderly carers. Expanding the focus on different kinds of carers is not only theoretically important, to fill the gaps, but also strategically, to increase equality. A care ethic informed by inclusive approaches can facilitate its theoretical relevance, empirical applicability and transformative potential in the context of growingly complex and multidimensional political challenges. The implications of more inclusive approaches to care are crucially important for current debates within social sciences, but also in terms of social policy.

The research here discussed has shown how care activities and responsibilities generate forms of group membership or status enhancement and consequent outcomes in terms of emotional energy production that alter people's emotional capital and emotional/social stratification. This in turn affects people's ability to successfully manage future interactions but also their ability to reconcile care work with work for the market. Reflexivity is the essential condition by which caregivers judge their care experiences as successful or unsuccessful. Without denying the importance of structural, economic and cultural factors in the reproduction of care-related inequality, this study claims that these factors need active mediation – the capacity and the willpower of individuals to act independently and to make their own choices – in order to be effective. Through their internal conversations, individuals reflect upon and mould their social and emotional situation in light of care-related tasks and concerns (Wiley, 1994; Archer, 2003, 2007). These inner dialogues govern caregivers' responses to social forces, their actual and potential patterns of social interaction, and whether they contribute to social inequality; an inequality that is based on the felt experience of care.

Acknowledging the intrinsic value of care and highlighting its potentially inclusive and self-empowering consequences does not mean giving voice to a romanticised view of the world or failing to recognise the draining aspects of care, but rather capitalising on care as a long-term investment and a resource. If the majority of the carers in this study experience care in terms of status inclusion and self-empowering processes, some however experience feelings of disconnectedness and powerlessness. The capitalisation of care can only be accomplished by facilitating the conditions under which care can become a self-empowering and productive experience and by reducing those under which it becomes a constraining, excluding or emotional-energy draining experience.

Creating the conditions for more caring, more just and more inclusive societies and acknowledging the role of all different types of carers (single and partnered/married; heterosexual and homosexual; involved in childcare or elderly care, etc.) represents the first step towards these ends. In doing that, we can also reduce the inequality connected to this fundamental activity. But all this, quite obviously, cannot be left to the individuals alone and their personal/private responsibilities.

References
Archer, M. (2003). *Structure, agency, and the internal conversation.* New York, NY: Cambridge University Press.
Archer, M. (2007). *Making our way through the world. Human reflexivity and social mobility.* Cambridge, United Kingdom: Cambridge University Press.
Barbalet, J. M. (2001). *Emotion, social theory, and social structure: A macrosociological approach.* Cambridge, United Kingdom: Cambridge University Press.
Barnes, M. (2012). *Care in everyday life: An ethic of care in practice.* Bristol, United Kingdom: Policy Press.
Clarke, V. (2007). Men not included? A critical psychology analysis of lesbian families and male influence in child rearing. *Journal of GLBT Family Studies, 3,* 309–349.

Clarke, V. (2008). From outsiders to motherhood to reinventing the family: Constructions of lesbian parenting in the psychological literature – 1886-2006. *Women's Studies International Forum, 31,* 118-128.

Collins, R. (2004). *Interaction ritual chains.* Princeton, NJ: Princeton University Press.

Dean, H. (2004). Reconceptualising dependency, responsibility and rights. In H. Dean (Ed.), *The ethics of welfare: Human rights, dependency and responsibility* (pp. 193-210). Bristol, United Kingdom: Policy Press.

Duncan, S., & Smith, D. P. (2006). Individualisation versus the geography of 'new' families. *21st Century Society: the Academy of Social Sciences Journal, 1*(2), 149-166.

Duncan, S., & Phillips, M. (2008). New families? Tradition and change in modern relationships. *British social attitudes: The 24th report.* London, United Kingdom: Sage.

Finch, J., & Groves, D. (Eds.). (1983). *A labor of love: Women, work and caring.* London, United Kingdom: Routledge.

Fisher, B., & Tronto, J. (1990). Toward a feminist theory of caring. In E. Abel & M. Nelson (Eds.), *Circles of care: Work and identity in women's lives* (pp. 35-62). New York: SUNY Press.

Folbre, N., & Nelson, J. A. (2000). For love or money or both? *Journal of Economic Perspectives, 14*(4), 123-140.

Gilligan, C. (1982). *In a different voice: Psychological theory and women's development.* Cambridge, MA: Harvard University Press.

Graham, H. (1983). Caring: A labour of love. In J. Finch & D. Groves (Eds.), *A labour of love: Women, work and caring* (pp. 13-30). London, United Kingdom: Routledge.

Graham, H. (1991). The concept of caring in feminist research: The case of domestic service, *Sociology, 25,* 61-78.

Held, V. (2006). *The ethics of care: Personal, political, and global*. Oxford, United Kingdom: Oxford University Press.

Himmelweit, S. (1999). Caring labor. *Annals, AAPPS, 561*(January), 27–38.

Hochschild, A. R. (2003). *The commercialization of intimate life: Notes from home and work*. Los Angeles: University of California Press.

Hochschild, A. R. (2012). *The outsourced self: Intimate life in market times*. New York, NY: Metropolitan Books.

Hochschild, A. R., & Ehrenreich, B. (Eds.). (2003). *Global woman: Nannies, maids and sex workers in the new economy*. New York, NY: Metropolitan Books.

Kantola, J. (2010). *Gender and the European Union*. Basingstoke, United Kingdom: Palgrave Macmillan.

Kemper, T. D. (1990). Social relations and emotions: A structural approach. In T. D. Kemper (Ed.), *Research agendas in the sociology of emotions* (pp. 207–237). New York: SUNY Press.

Kittay, E. (1999). *Love's labor: Essays on women, equality, and dependency*. New York, NY: Routledge.

Kittay, E., & Feder, E. (2002). *The subject of care: Feminist perspectives on dependency*. Lanham, MD: Rowman and Littlefield.

Kittay, E. F. (2007). Beyond autonomy and paternalism: The caring transparent self. In T. Nys, Y. Denier & T. Vandervelde (Eds.), *Autonomy & paternalism: Reflections on the theory and practice of health care* (pp. 23-70). Leuven, Belgium: Peeters Publishing.

Knijn, T., & Kremer, M. (1997). Gender and the caring dimension of welfare states: Toward inclusive citizenship. *Social Politics: International Studies in Gender, State and Society, 4*(3), 328–361.

Leira, A. (1994). Concepts of caring: Loving, thinking, and doing. *Social Service Review, 68,* 185–201.

Lewis, J. (2006). Work-family reconciliation, equal opportunities and social policies: the interpretation of policy trajectories at the EU level and the meaning of gender equality. *Journal of European Public Policy* 13(3), 400–437.

Nelson, F. (2007). Mother tongues: The discursive journeys of lesbian and heterosexual women into motherhood. *Journal of GLBT Family Studies, 3,* 223–265.

Noddings, N. (1984). *Caring: A feminine approach to ethics and moral education.* Berkeley: University of California Press.

Patterson, C. J., & Riskind, R. G. (2010). To be a parent: Issues in family formation among gay and lesbian adults. *Journal of GLBT Family Studies, 6,* 326–340.

Pratesi, A. (2011). The productivity of care: Contextualizing care in situated interaction and shedding light on its latent purposes. *Ethics and Social Welfare, 5*(2), 123–137.

Pratesi, A. (2012). A respectable scandal: Gay parenthood, emotional dynamics, and social change. *Journal of GLBT Family Studies, 8*(5), 305–333.

Roseneil, S., & Budgeon, S. (2004). Cultures of intimacy and care beyond 'the family': Personal life and social change in the early 21st century. *Current Sociology, 52*(2), 135–159.

Roth, S. (Ed.). (2008). *Gender politics in the expanding European Union: Mobilization, inclusion, exclusion.* New York, NY: Berghahn Books.

Ruddick, S. (1998). Care as labor and relationship. In J. G. Haber & M. S. Halfon (Eds.), *Norms and values: Essays on the work of Virginia Held.* (pp. 3–25). Lanham, MD: Rowman and Littlefield.

Stratigaki, M. (2004). The cooptation of gender concepts in EU policies: The case of "reconciliation of work and family".

Social Politics: International Studies in Gender, State & Society, 11(1), 30–56.

Thomas, C. (1993). De-constructing concepts of care, *Sociology*, 27, 649–669.

Tronto, J. (1987). Beyond gender difference to a theory of care. *Signs*, 12, 644–663.

Tronto, J. (1994). *Moral boundaries: A political argument for an ethic of care*. New York, NY: Routledge.

Ungerson, C. (1995). Gender, cash, and informal care: European perspectives and dilemmas. *Journal of Social Politics*, 24(1), 31–52.

Ungerson, C. (1997). Social politics and the commodification of care. *Social Politics*, 4(3), 362–381.

Waerness, K. (1984). The rationality of care. *Economic and Industrial Democracy*, 5, 185–211.

Weicht, B. (2010). Embracing dependency: Rethinking (in)dependence in the discourse of care. *The Sociological Review*, 58(s2), 205–224.

Weston, K. (1997). *Families we choose: Lesbians, gays, kinship*. New York, NY: Columbia University Press.

White, J. A., & Tronto, J. C. (2004). Political practices of care: Needs and rights. *Ratio Juris*, 17(4), 425–453.

Wiley, N. (1994). *The semiotic self*. Chicago, IL: University of Chicago Press.

Zelizer, V. A. (2005). *The purchase of intimacy*. Princeton, NJ: Princeton University Press.

CHAPTER 2

THE CORONER'S INQUEST AND VISCERAL REACTIONS: CONSIDERING THE IMPACT OF SELF-INFLICTED DEATHS ON THE HEALTH AND SOCIAL CARE PROFESSIONAL

Karen Corteen, Paul Taylor and Sharon Morley

This chapter presents a discussion of the potential impact of participation in the Coroner's Inquest for health and social care professionals.[1] Through the process of the Coroner's Inquest and the public and media interest in the deaths of those under the care and supervision of health and social care services, in particular self-inflicted deaths, we locate the health and social care professional in a position of potential vulnerability and primary, secondary and tertiary victimisation. It is suggested that health and social care professionals experience victimisation as a result of experiencing self-inflicted deaths and iatrogenic harm (an inadvertent and adverse effect) in the aftermath through visible participation in the official processes of the state. The experience of the health and social care professional is situated within an analytical context of victimology, a lens by which unconventional harms can become known or observed. In doing so, we question the usefulness of the hierarchy of

---

[1] Health and social care professionals here come to mean those working for government agencies and also private sector companies that deliver care, treatment and/or supervision to members of the public and those detained by the state. These include registered practitioners (registered mental health nurses and psychiatrists in particular), social workers and those in roles allied to these professions.

victimisation and we offer a revisionist approach to understanding the impact of media reporting of coronial inquests into self-inflicted deaths on those individuals in health and social care occupations. Importantly a distinction is made between public service workers[2] who make regrettable mistakes (misfeasance) and those that engage in intentional wrongdoing and unprofessional practices (malfeasance).

The death of a family member, partner or friend is a tragic event and signals an interruption in the usual life course of that person, often through the experiencing of personal and familial grief. However, as Biddle (2003) remarks, the death of a person can, at times, become a *public* event rather than just a *private* tragedy through mandatory requirements to engage with the officialdom of the state during the Coroner's Inquest procedures. Establishing the cause of death and the circumstances surrounding it are the principal goals of the Coroner's Inquest – a process that will involve multiple actors. Whilst the Coroner's Inquest may go some way in answering the uncertainty surrounding the person's death, it also carries further significance for those involved, not least in the prolonged nature of this official process.

Involvement in coronial matters does not end at the participation of family members and significant others; indeed as Rutty (2000) indicates, public service workers such as nurses are likely at some point in their career to be involved in coronial matters. Participation as a witness in the Coroner's Inquest of public service workers involves official scrutiny, for

---

[2] Whilst our primary focus here has been with occupations within the health and social care discipline – a public service – equally our analysis may be applied to other occupations sharing similar mandates and responsibilities, for example probation officers and probation work.

example the evidence provided (e.g. records, recalling decision-making) will be subject to official examination by the Coroner and unofficial scrutiny by those observing (e.g. those in the gallery and media audiences). Whilst liability is not apportioned through the Coroner's Inquest in the legal sense, the inquisitorial process may unveil perceived negligence, missed opportunities, unprofessional practices or poor service standards and propel these sentiments into the public domain.

Self-inflicted deaths are relatively common events (Foley & Kelly, 2007) and as such those involved in occupations which administer care or supervision will inevitably become involved in the legal processes that surround unexpected deaths (Green, 1993). Whilst the deceased's family and friends may be observed to experience the direct and primary victimising effects of loss, those professionals who have been active in the role of care, treatment and/or supervision may also experience a sense of loss, albeit less observable.

Indeed, some have sought to unveil the potential hazards of this legal process. The question has been asked whether a Coroner is necessarily the best informed person to oversee inquests into self-inflicted deaths, particularly those where the deceased had mental health problems, given they have less experience than the practitioners involved in such cases. Hobbs (2001) highlights how Coroners can come to odd conclusions particularly if they have not employed a practitioner to assist them. Furthermore, the ability for public service workers to avoid 'mistakes' in the normal pursuit of their duties has been deliberated. Public service workers, such as health and social care professionals, are semi-autonomous practitioners, that is their work is heavily anchored to, and embedded in, normal contexts in which people perform work under conditions of resource constraints and outcome uncertainty (Wood et al., 2010 cited in Dekker, 2013), which may not be taken into account in Coroner's verdicts, and thus a fair adjudication may not be reached. In a similar vein, media reporting of Coroner's findings and verdicts may omit significant occupational contexts in which self-inflicted deaths and those experiencing them take place. It is clear then that such legal practices do not exist in a vacuum, rather there are a number of potential complex subjectivities and consequences that are intrinsic in this practice of state officialdom.

In the area of health and social care, self-inflicted deaths have been conceived as an occupational hazard and a common occurrence (Chemtob, Bauer, Hamada, Pelowski, & Muraoka, 1989; Landeen, 1988; Campbell & Fahy, 2002; Yousaf, Hawthorne, & Sedgwick, 2002). The literature reviewing the impact of service user self-inflicted deaths on health and social care professionals is extensive. The themes of blame and responsibility are articulated across many empirical studies (see for example, Dewar, Eagles, Klein, Gray, & Alexander, 2000; Foley & Kelly, 2007 for a review of the literature). According to Midence, Gregory, and Stanley (1996) feelings of negative judgments over professional decision-making are common and that there are mixed emotions and responses including "sadness, frustration, shock, fear, anger and guilt" (p. 116). Indeed, not only are professionals subject to the personal emotional consequences, but also report feelings of being the subject of 'witch hunts' and being used as a 'scapegoat' during the investigation of the death (Alexander, Klein, Gray, Dewar, & Eagles, 2000). However, when turning attention to the impact of coronial processes among health and social care professionals, there is a dearth of literature.

The impact of service-user self-inflicted deaths is therefore twofold. Empirical evidence points towards both the *personal* and *professional* significance of a self-inflicted death, with its impact being felt in the *personal* lives of practitioners and changes being made in *professional* practice (Linke, Wojciak, & Day, 2002). Furthermore, behaviour changes are evident in clinical practice as a result of service user suicides in addition to cautionary approaches and the avoidance of certain therapeutic engagements or interactions (Linke et al., 2002). Due to the nature of risk responsibility and management, a vicarious traumatisation may also be apparent among such professionals whereby the traumatic event of the service user death has been noted as contributing to the development of conditions such as post-traumatic stress disorder (Gitlin, 1999) and depression (Jones, 1987) among psychiatrists.

Official procedures surrounding incidences of service-user self-inflicted deaths vary, but may involve external scrutiny (for example, coronial procedures) in addition to internal organisational procedures (such as root-cause analyses). Processes of investigation, whilst typically undertaken in a timely manner, may take several months to complete. Moreover, complaints and litigation may extend the case beyond the decision of the Coroner's Inquest. Formal inquiries into service user deaths represent the convergence of professional medical expertise, legal protocols and bureaucratic process (see Taylor, Corteen, & Morley, 2013). It is these multiple dimensions of engaging with the authority of the state coupled with the emotional impact upon the professional(s) of the service user's death that all serve to problematise the process of investigation. For example, in a study of consultant psychiatrists, Alexander et al. (2000) report that legal and disciplinary procedures could be viewed unfavourably, advocating that such undertakings should be completed within a constructive climate. Also, in a study of mental health community teams, Linke et al. (2002) posit that it is necessary for senior staff to publicly acknowledge how disturbing self-inflicted deaths can be for mental health teams, the aim of which is to avoid such circumstances being overlooked, trivialised, or being viewed as a normative occupational reality.

A small body of literature has sought to examine the significance of media representations of service user suicides. Unsurprisingly perhaps, research has unveiled that selective media reporting of these tragedies exacerbated negative feelings and emotions among those public service workers involved in official processes. Media coverage of deaths and their inquiries/inquests are viewed as distressing for public service workers (Alexander et al., 2000). Likewise, Midence, Gregory, and Stanley (1996) report that the way in which the media may report a patient suicide leaves nurses feeling personally attacked and feeling personally responsible for the tragedy. Moreover, media coverage was reported to lack balance and a comprehensive understanding of the circumstances leading to clinical staff feeling powerless to defend themselves (Midence et al., 1996).

The Coroner's Process, Inquest and Verdict
In the United Kingdom there is a mandatory duty to refer unnatural deaths, deaths involving violence and deaths that occur whilst the person is in the care of the state to the Coroner. Deaths will be reported to the Coroner often when the cause of death is uncertain or unexplained; something that has seen little change over its history. Coroners are the responsible individuals who can determine whether the cause and circumstances of the death can be explained and decide whether further investigation is required. The Coroner may order a post-mortem and if this procedure fails to conclude that the death was the result of natural causes (or that the death occurred whilst the individual was in the custody of the state), a Coroner's Inquest will be called (see Jennings &

The Coroner's Inquest and Visceral Reactions

Barraclough, 1980). During 2010, 31,000 inquests were opened on the 230,600 deaths reported to Coroners (Ministry of Justice, 2011).

In a small number of cases (for example where the death has occurred in prison or police custody, or where the death is reportable under separate legislation), a jury may return a verdict, however, usual practice involves the Coroner sitting alone. There is no legal requirement for the Coroner's verdict to be returned in any particular form. Historically, Coroners have returned shortened verdicts such as 'natural causes', 'open verdicts', 'misadventure', 'unlawful killing' and 'suicide' (returning a *felo de se* (or 'self-murder') verdict only accounts for 11% of the 29,400 verdict-returning inquests during 2010 (Ministry of Justice, 2011)). The Ministry of Justice (2011) and Hill and Cook for the Office for National Statistics (2011) both report an increasing trend of unclassified verdicts standing at 14% in 2010 in contrast to just 1% in 2001. As Gunnell, Hawton, and Kapur (2011) illustrate, "a growing number of coroners have summarized their inquest findings with a narrative verdict which records, in several sentences, how, and in what circumstances, the death occurred rather than giving a short form verdict" (p. 1). The narrative verdict therefore becomes an important instrument in directing the attention of the court and the wider public to matters that the Coroner believes are of public concern. Such verdicts allow for central issues to be raised, and whilst not a liability apportioning exercise (in the legal sense), can illuminate inadequacies in processes or procedures of responsible agencies. In such cases, supplementary comments will invariably impact badly on those who were responsible for the care, treatment and/or supervision of the deceased at the time of death.

Self-Inflicted Deaths, Coronial Processes and Harm
The legal procedures and a Coroner's Inquest can be a source of distress for the family of the deceased (Hawton & Simkin, 2003) and for public service professionals (Alexander et al., 2000). Understanding such distress among family members has received some attention (Barraclough & Shepherd, 1977) whilst the literature discussing the aftermath and effects of suicide among health and social care professionals tends to ignore the impact of legal procedures (Taylor, Corteen, & Morley, 2013). Much discussion of this topic centres upon the practical responsibilities of the professional (see Campbell & Fahy, 2002) rather than the impact of official coronial procedures (Taylor et al., 2013). Indeed, as Ruben (1990) astutely reminds us, professionals may experience comparable feelings of loss to the family. It is possible then that for the health and social care professional, the feelings of guilt, self-blame, responsibility and grief (those similar to those felt by the family – see Barraclough & Shepherd, 1976) may become more intense and enduring as a consequence of legal participation as a witness. The distress felt by public service professionals called as witnesses is therefore an important dimension of the coronial process to consider and it is crucial to do so victimologically. The intensification of one or all of the aforementioned feelings can be traced to the 'visibility' of the health and social care professional within the inquest procedure. They may have prepared statements that will be read, be questioned by the Coroner in the Court and be subject to comments from the deceased's family. The initial self-inflicted death and the Coroner's Inquest can induce a plethora of negative emotions within the health and social care professional. As such, these two events (the death itself and the Coroner's Inquest) that they become subject to (without choice) can be considered as potentially harmful and

victimising. In light of this, the study of such circumstances within a framework of harm and victimisation has the potential to elucidate the experience of the health and social care professional further (Taylor et al., 2013).

Self-Inflicted Deaths and News Reporting
Whilst the experience of the actual coronial process may be distressing for all involved, the propagation of information drawn from the inquest via media reporting may also inflame the situation. These publicised representations may be distressing for relatives, but also for practitioners involved as witnesses. Much research in this area analyses the news reporting of self-inflicted deaths and aligns its focus on the potential for careless reporting to encourage copycat behaviours or what is known as the Werther Effect (see Goldney, 2001; Pirkis, Blood, Beautrais, Burgess, & Skehans, 2006; Dare, Andriessen, Nordentoft, Meier, Huisman, & Pirkis, 2011). Little is known of the potential impact on public service workers (acting as witnesses) of media reporting during and following a Coroner's Inquest. This area is potentially significant as sentiments of responsibility may be carried from the confines of the court into the public arena under the auspices of public interest in the case. In such instances witnesses are publicly identified by name. Furthermore, media imperatives or news values such as threshold, predictability, simplification, individualism, risk, proximity and newsworthiness (see Jewkes, 2011) may result in misrepresentations of events and public sector workers, including those in health and social care occupations. Important complexities, contexts and nuances may not be encapsulated in media reporting, particularly those cases reported by the tabloid or popular press.

Media censorship is a highly contested and contestable area and guidance on appropriate suicide media reporting has been challenged for the potential to stifle free-press (Herman, 2000). In what authors have termed as 'risk news' (Blood, Pirkis, & Holland, 2007), the reporting of suicide is not benign, rather the decision to report and the character of the report are influenced by a number of factors. In an appreciation of the literature surrounding 'risk news' reporting, Blood et al. (2007) draw together a number of influences, namely: "the nature of the risk, the size, timescale, novelty, and human face" (p. 65), in conjunction with organisational factors, journalistic routines and the cultural or geographical proximity of the event. Influence on the media reporting of self-inflicted deaths also potentially comes from more official sources of guidance, for example the World Health Organization (WHO) and the International Association for Suicide Prevention (IASP). Broadly these guidelines call for accurate, responsible and ethical representations. A number of countries such as Australia, Canada and the United Kingdom have developed their own specific resources (see Pirkis et al., 2006 for an overview). Importantly many of these sources include the recommendation that journalists consider the aftermath of a self-inflicted death – that is taking care and showing respect to those bereaved (Pirkis et al., 2006).

Journalistic and editorial judgements over the reporting of suicide have been further interrogated by Pirkis et al. (2007). Through a textual analysis of 515 Australian newspaper reports describing events of suicidal behaviour, the authors constructed a number of themes including:

> [S]uicides by older people are, relatively more likely to be reported than suicides by younger people; suicides by females take reporting prominence over suicides by males; and suicides by violent or dramatic methods appear to be

The Coroner's Inquest and Visceral Reactions

considered particularly newsworthy (Pirkis et al., 2007, p. 281).

It is this final point that seems cogent in the debates to be had in this chapter. Foresight of the potentially deleterious effects of suicide reporting is perhaps less well understood in available research and analyses. The extract below, from a local UK newspaper reporting on a Coroner's Inquest in 2013 highlights such an individualising approach to reporting:[3]

> The social worker responsible for looking after teenager [deceased name] was not qualified when she took over his case – and was on a week-long training course that ended the day he died. ... [social worker's name] appeared at the inquest into the death of 14-year-old [deceased's name] ... on Monday afternoon and was questioned until 4pm on Tuesday.

Similarly in another Coroner's Inquest in 2010, a newspaper reports that:

> A nurse yesterday told an inquest she had failed to meet the professional duty of care due to a patient who was found hanged on a hospital mental unit. ... [nurse's name] told the hearing how she had failed to properly monitor the care plan for [deceased's name], who was found dead at the [hospital name] ... [deceased's name], 48, ... was found hanged with a bed sheet during his stay on the 20-patient [ward name] ward on January 14.

Again, the individualising character of news reporting is shown here from a report in 2011:

---

[3] Whilst these sources are available in the public domain, the authors here have elected to omit the details of the original source to avoid further identification of those individually involved.

> Mental health teams were too busy to assess a girl found hanged even though they knew she was at risk a month before her death, an inquest heard. ... [city name] council social worker, [social worker's name], who was part of the children's mental health team, explained how he had received the referral, but he had so much other work that he did not have time to follow it up.

Selective reporting may impact severely on the professionals involved. The nuances of the circumstances surrounding a case may be lost and whilst failures of a process, professional judgement or even negligence may be relevant, the burden of responsibility may well be carried unduly by the professional(s) present in the Court. Suggestions that organisational processes may have failed the deceased (for example levels of supervision, etc.) may be common, however where news reporting is conducted in an individualising manner, then the responsibility for what may be defects in systems or processes is shouldered by the professional themselves (who may not have sufficient professional autonomy to have prevented the self-inflicted death). Responsibility here refers to being called to account for one's actions (Onyett, 1995; Herman, Trauer, & Warnock, 2002). However, the expectation that professionals are always able to accurately assess risk, and the idea that 'professionalism' is confused with 'infallibility' is unfair as it is impossible to identify and eliminate risk entirely (Stickley & Felton, 2006).

Negligence and Liability
The Tort of negligence is legal terminology used in civil justice cases of negligence. Increasingly public sector services, in particular health services, are subject to civil law cases being brought where there is question over the standard of care provided or where harm occurred through actions or an

omission of actions. A 'balance of probabilities' principle is applied to cases of negligence and for the case to be favoured to the claimant, four aspects must be proved: a duty of care was owed to them (for example, a service user under a professional's care/supervision); the duty was breached (for example, not acting in a manner aligned to that of a competent/skilled professional); harm was caused (establishing that harm resulted from a breach of duty); causation (showing the causal link between breach of duty and resultant harm) (see Cornock, 2011 for an overview). If the defendant is found liable then the court will ask the defendant to pay compensation to the claimant. In June 2013, the National Health Service (NHS) costs for negligence claims was forecasted to reach £19 billion, around one fifth of the total NHS budget (Donnelly, 2013).

It is challenging to discern the levels of litigation within public services linked with service-user self-inflicted deaths (however see Mordue, Weatherby, Weatherby, & Pearson, 2012 for an overview of litigation claims across a generalised psychiatric patient journey). Yet, a nationally reported case related to the death of Bryan Jobson has brought into sharp focus circumstances where not only civil claims of negligence may be pursued, but also criminal charges against public service personnel. This case also highlights the "shifting categories and definitions of what constitutes as acceptable behaviour" (Dekker, 2013, p. 63), with professional 'mistakes', where no criminal intent is evident, becoming increasingly more likely to be prosecuted under criminal law.

The Coroner's Inquest into the death of Bryan Jobson, a man under the care of a Crisis Resolution Home Treatment team in Leeds, who hanged himself in his own home, criticised mental health workers for leaving Mr Jobson alone despite observing a ligature in his property and being concerned about his state of mind. A news report on the *Mail Online* also revealed that two Mental Health workers had been interviewed under police caution to investigate whether a charge of Gross Negligence Manslaughter could be brought (Hartley-Parkinson & Nolan, 2013). Gross Negligence Manslaughter, a form of Involuntary Manslaughter, is said to exist where the defendant commits a lawful act in such a way as to render the actions criminal. Similar to the Tort of negligence, the prosecution must establish that: the defendant owed a duty of care; there was a breach of that duty of care; the breach caused harm (in this case death); and that the breach was sufficient (in the opinion of the jury) to constitute a crime.

Through this process of criminalisation of human error, the management of public anxiety becomes visible. This is achieved by highlighting not only the moral, but also the legal boundaries of acceptable and unacceptable professional behaviour (Dekker, 2013). However, while criminalisation may demonstrate that these boundaries exist it has a detrimental impact on the management of risk and safety. As discussed by a number of commentators (see Dekker, 2013) it impedes independent safety investigations. More importantly, it promotes fear among professionals resulting in negative consequences in that professionals may try to cover up mistakes resulting in a decline in the voluntary reporting of mistakes and errors. As Chapman (2009 cited in Dekker, 2013, p. 61) asserts, "[p]ractising under the threat of prosecution can only serve to hide errors" (p. 61).

A further consequence of this criminalisation process is the lack of responsibility accepted by organisations whose employees make mistakes, with individual professionals shouldering the blame. This individualising of responsibility and blame fails to take into account the structural and regulatory constraints within which health and social care professionals operate, and also "oversimplifies the complexity of contributory events" (Dekker, 2013, p. 65). It may also influence how professionals provide care and/or supervision, thus placing professionals' individual self-protection before the needs of service users, resulting in defensive practices (Chiplin, Bos, Harris, & Codye, 1998; Mullen, Admiraal, & Trevena, 2008).

Liability, be that criminal or civil, weighs heavy on those professionals involved in managing service users who pose risks to themselves. Indeed, for some professions, they may also be in breach of professional codes of conduct (see Huxley-Binns, 2008). It is clear then that the tragic event of a service user death has the potential to impact greatly upon those involved in the delivery of care, treatment and/or supervision. Feelings of grief are likely to be experienced at the loss of the deceased, however this is then potentially worsened through the processes that may follow. Evidence-giving at the Coroner's Inquest, selective and individualised news reporting, internal investigations, inquiries by professional bodies, civil litigation claims and the potential for criminal prosecutions in some cases all combine to make this a highly emotional, traumatic and professionally discrediting experience for practitioners.

Self-Inflicted Deaths and the Coronial Inquest – A Victimising Event

Self-inflicted deaths of service users predominantly provoke visceral public reactions. We suggest that the Coronial inquest into self-inflicted deaths should be considered as a victimising event borne out of the coronial process and verdict, exacerbated by its public nature and media reporting. The latter can reinforce, provoke and whip up existing visceral public reactions, which can result in health and social care professionals feeling and experiencing harm and victimisation. In order to look at these contentions through a victimological lens the notions of 'victim' and 'victimisation' including the multi-levels of victimisation have to be discussed.

The use of terms such as 'victim' and 'victimisation' has a firm history in the study of the impact of crime (Fisher & Lab, 2010; Karmen, 2013). Indeed victims of conventional crime permeate and dominate the criminal justice system, victim activism, victimological and criminological literature, politics, official policies and practices, the media and the public imagination. Subsequently victimologists, victim activists, criminologists, criminal justice practitioners, politicians, the media and the public predominantly envisage "victimisation in terms of an obvious perpetrator, victim, act of victimisation, and a clear intent to harm" (Corteen & Corteen, 2012, p. 49).

Victimologists do, however, recognise that not all victims, including victims of crime, are publicly, officially and politically perceived, received and responded to as such. Victims are constructed along a continuum from that of the 'deserving' victim to that of the 'undeserving' victim. The "deserving" or "ideal victim" (Christie, 1986, p. 18) comprises 'innocent' individuals who are readily bequeathed legitimate or *true* victim status because they are free of guilt, culpability, blame and risk. Public, political, and media sympathy, compassion and support are forthcoming and unwavering for the vulnerable 'ideal' victim. 'Undeserving' victims however, are denied victim status, media attention and public and political support and sympathy. The dominance of the notion of an 'ideal' victim of crime who is obviously and legitimately a true victim, with a visible perpetrator (intent on causing them harm or injury) results in the omission, neglect or even negation of a range of harms and victimising events including occupational-related harm and victimisation (Corteen & Corteen, 2012). Health and social care workers and other public service workers whose compulsory participation in the public coronial process and who may be misrepresented in the media reporting of it are victims who are "not in keeping with common-sense thinking and mainstream academic victimology or victim activism" (Corteen & Corteen, 2012, p. 49). The phrase "Victimological Other" (Walklate, 2007a, p. 52) has been coined to "refer to the way in which victimology makes groups of people more likely to be included as victims rather than others" (Davies, 2011, p. 196). It encapsulates the victim that "falls outside of the normative imagery of theory and practice" (Walklate, 2007a, p. 53).

Therefore, increasingly a focus on victims beyond conventional victims of crime, together with an emphasis on harm, has led to an analytical lens and a way of 'seeing' harms that a broad range of 'invisible' victims experience (Quinney, 1972; Elias, 1985; Corteen & Corteen, 2012). Thus *who* is a 'victim' and *what* 'victimisation' entails have "been debated and contested within victimology since its inception, accumulating in a vibrant discussion in the latter part of the twentieth century" (Taylor et al., 2013, p. 32). Radical and critical victimologists challenge the confinement of the victim within the parameters of criminal law (Goodey, 2005) and the conceptual straitjacket of crime and the criminal law has been critiqued (Barton, Corteen, Scott, & Whyte, 2007). A radical and critical victimological approach has established that a victim is someone who is harmed or killed, intentionally or unintentionally, as a result of an act, event or situation that is not necessarily criminal and wherein there may or may not be a perpetrator. Thus the harm or victimisation experienced by those in health and social care occupations as a result of self-inflicted deaths of service users, and subsequent coronial inquests, can be observed through a more critical, imaginative and encompassing victimological lens.

With regard to the victimising effects of the coronial inquest and verdict in terms of its public nature and media reporting of it, health and social care professionals are the victimological other. To some extent this is perhaps understandable as at the root of professional (rhetorically at least), political and public interest in, and visceral reactions to, self-inflicted deaths, are the people who have died and their families and friends, some of whom are seen predominantly as 'deserving' victims because of their proximity to the tragedies. Health and social care professionals however, when they do come under the professional, political and public gaze, rightly or wrongly, may be put in the frame as in some way culpable and thus blameworthy for the service user's death as a result of a 'mistake', omission, neglect or unprofessional practices. Thus, their victim status is unacknowledged or questionable. The victimisation of health and social care professionals as a result of 'inferred' responsibility for service user deaths "has largely gone unrecognized in academia and in government policy" (Taylor et al., 2013, p. 32). We are not stating that health and social care professionals are intentionally targeted, innocent, true victims in the traditional or conventional sense but we are making a case that they do experience victimisation as a result of Coroner's Inquests, verdicts and media reporting. We are arguing that as a result of this process, health and social care professionals can inadvertently be stigmatised and rendered relatively helpless, vulnerable and disempowered. At the same time, they have little recourse to redress or capacity to address their potential negative representation or misrepresentation in the inquest and the verdict – especially if it is a narrative verdict – and in media and public visceral reactions. In order to begin this quest we need to look at the multi-levels of victimisation as established within and without victimology.

Most notably, victimological scholars have sought to distinguish between different types of victimisation. The concepts of 'primary', 'secondary' and 'tertiary' victimisation have been widely applied (Spalek, 2006; Walklate, 2007b; Burgess, Regehr, & Roberts, 2011; Davies, 2011). This is in order to illuminate the nature of harm and suffering and it has led to what is often referred to as a 'victim hierarchy' (Spalek, 2006; Davies, 2011). That said, in victimological literature and elsewhere terms such as 'primary', 'secondary' and tertiary' are not always interpreted and applied in a uniform fashion. We argue here that clarity is needed when using and applying these concepts to *victims* and *victimisation*. In discussing self-inflicted deaths and official legal processes, we utilise and unpack these concepts and we try to do so with precision in order to ensure clarity and to make victimisation – hitherto unobserved – observable.

In the main the concept of a 'primary' *victim* refers to "those that experience harm directly" (Davies, 2011, p. 194). Based on Selvin and Wolfgang's (1964 in Burgess et al., 2011) explanation of primary victims, such individuals are a "targeted or personalized victim" (Burgess et al., 2011, p. 67), for example the intended person who is actually killed or directly hurt or affected (Karmen, 2001; Burgess et al., 2011; Davies, 2011). In this conceptualisation family, friends or witnesses of the victimisation who do not experience harm directly may be referred to as 'secondary' victims (Karmen, 2001; Burgess et al., 2011; Davies, 2011). Across academic literature, media representations and mental health campaigners' rhetoric there is a tenacious willingness to conceive service users who take their own lives as 'victims'. Thus their status as primary victim is predominantly assumed in the public imagination. As direct, primary victims they are (usually) the sole recipients of the act and its consequences, experiencing their effects first-hand. We too recognise this and in our exploration of health and social care professionals as victims it is not our intention to undermine or detract from the deceased and their family and friends. Nor do we wish to diminish or minimise service users' suffering as a result of the primary victimisation they endured.

We do, however, think it is important to look at the victimisation of health and social care professionals in the event of a self-inflicted death and in particular the victimisation experienced as a result of the coronial process and media reporting. Spalek (2006) rightly comments that:

> Whilst the terms 'primary', 'secondary' and 'tertiary' suggest that there is some sort of hierarchy in the level of suffering experienced, it cannot be assumed that secondary and tertiary victims necessarily suffer less trauma than primary victims, since secondary and tertiary victims can also face significant, physical, psychological and emotional pain (p. 13).

The issue here is to be clear in the distinction between a primary *victim* and primary *victimisation*. Thus whilst health and social care professionals are not primary victims in that they may not constitute the personalised, direct, target of service-users' self-inflicted deaths (and, arguably, this is debatable), they may experience primary victimisation; that is, the loss of a service user in their care or under their supervision has a primary harmful impact.

Deheegher (2008) suggests that primary victimisation can occur among those who witness the suicide or who are "confronted with the potentially traumatogenic factors of the suicide" (p. 155). We agree with Deheegher's (2008) inclusion

The Coroner's Inquest and Visceral Reactions

of witnesses in this discussion of primary victimisation. That said, the extent to whether or not public service workers exposed to, or involved in, a service user's death do experience primary victimisation cannot be adequately established here due to the shortage of studies and commentary on this. Yet, there are significant signs that this may be the case, which in turn raises concerns regarding the responses and support that are, or are not, as the case may be, in place for health and social care professionals and other public service workers when they are subjected to, or are involved in, service-user self-inflicted deaths. Arguably the case for secondary victimisation is somewhat stronger – it is to this victimological concept that we now turn our attention.

The phrase "secondary victimisation" is generally used in terms of "two distinct meanings": those "indirectly harmed" (family, friends and witnesses as already indicated above) and those whose feelings and experiences of victimisation are "exacerbated" (Davies, 2011, pp. 194–195). The first meaning of secondary victimisation, as has been illustrated, is used to describe the indirect or removed experience of victimisation on the part of other persons than the targeted or intended personalised primary victim (Karmen, 2001; Burgess et al., 2011; Davies, 2011).

The second meaning of secondary victimisation is that of being 're-victimised', which, according to Davies (2011), is the "more accurate meaning" (p. 195). Thus, during the aftermath of victimisation, a victim may experience secondary victimisation as a result of insensitive, inappropriate and even damaging responses to the victimisation and victim on the part of others, including victim blaming. Advertent and inadvertent inappropriate state responses to victimisation can be systemic (Davies, 2011). The often-used example to explain this idea or experience is the secondary victimisation of rape victims as a result of insensitive practices within the criminal justice system. It can also be used to encapsulate problems following the initial victimisation such as anxiety, trauma, fear, long-term pain or impairment as a result of sustained injuries. In the context of crime and criminal justice secondary victimisation is sometimes referred to as post-crime victimisation or double victimisation.

In the case of self-inflicted deaths, family and friends of the deceased and health and social care professionals may be affected by secondary victimisation in two ways. First, as a result of the immediate victimising event and second, as a result of the coronial process and its media coverage. With regard to the first, as noted above, there is ample evidence that self-inflicted deaths of service users have a negative impact on health and social care professionals. For example professionals have altered their practices including undertaking cautionary approaches (Linke, Wojciak, & Day, 2002). Gitlin (1999) points out that professionals can experience post-traumatic stress disorder after experiencing a traumatic incident. It could be argued that changes in practices and behaviour and medical conditions such as post-traumatic stress disorder may be evidence of secondary victimisation in that they are a response to the initial victimising event that they witnessed or where involved in.

Further, in the aftermath when practitioners feel that they are being personally attacked, blamed and negatively judged they experience emotions such as sadness, fear, shock and guilt (Midence et al., 1996). They may also feel they are the subject of a 'witch-hunt' and scapegoating (Alexander et al., 2000). Thus the public coronial process, verdict and subsequent political, public, and media visceral reaction may exacerbate these emotions and may even result in primary victimisation as in the case when public sector workers harm and even kill themselves in response to public negativity, including naming and shaming.

Professionals may also suffer as a result of a spoiled identity. A study conducted by Scott, Hirschinger, Cox, et al. (2009) found that professionals who had made a 'mistake' believed they had failed their patient, that they had "second guessed their clinical skills, knowledge base and career choices" (cited in Dekker, 2013, p. 65), resulting in professionals suffering from depression, anxiety, stress, guilt and self-blame. In some cases professionals changed careers voluntarily, changed location or professional role, or continued to practise but were ever conscious of the 'mistake' they had made. In cases where practitioners were disciplined as a result of the 'mistake', they faced difficulties in finding employment in the sector. Arguably some professionals who have made a 'mistake' suffer personally and professionally as a result of this.

It is important that professionals are accountable and that if they behave unprofessionally that they are appropriately and effectively disciplined. Wrongdoers in positions of power should be subjected to mechanisms of power and control, as are the vulnerable and marginalised powerless members of society. As Barton et al., (2007) rightly comment "[h]arms caused by negligence or caused by omissions – harms produced as a result of non-decisions – were largely exempt from the system of criminal punishment" (pp. 202–203). However, we would differentiate between professionals who engage in complete wrongdoing, unequivocal illegal activity or intentional professional misconduct – *malfeasance* – and professionals who inadvertently make a mistake that is not illegal or unintentionally perform improperly whilst carrying out their duties – *misfeasance*. For example, professionals – whatever their occupation – who engage in "state organizational deviance" or "human rights violations" (Green & Ward, 2000, p. 110) and states of denial (Cohen, 2000) such as those involved in the perversion and denial of justice in the Hillsborough case warrant a different discussion and response to those deemed to have committed misfeasance. A mistaken failure to identify a preventable or unpreventable self-inflicted death is very different to the systematic and blatantly forced (and otherwise) alteration and suppression of statements and vilification of victims and the bereaved in the aftermath of Hillsborough (for a more in-depth analysis of Hillsborough see Scraton, Jemphrey, & Coleman, 1995; McGovern & McDougall, 1996; the Hillsborough Independent Panel, 2012).

In addition, with regard to criminal punishment in an adversarial system, theoretically at least, guilt of the defendant has to be established beyond reasonable doubt via clear rules of evidence and the defendant has the right to legal representation and the opportunity to defend themselves. The Coroner's Inquest is a slightly different animal – whilst health and social care professionals and public service workers whose professional conduct is under scrutiny have the right to representation they are arguably more vulnerable and "the least able to challenge verdicts that make … 'inferred' statements of blame and responsibility" (Taylor et al., 2013, p. 33). In cases such as that discussed above, professionals who made a 'mistake' – misfeasance – suffered internal organisational troubles, behaviour and professional role modification and external problems (such as spoiled reputation and misrepresentation), some of which should be acknowledged as secondary victimisation.

Whilst some victims may feel a sense of justice and/or retribution or revenge in the public declaration and negative judgement of an individual professional and their 'mistake(s)', for the individual professional themselves whatever their occupation, the coronial process, verdict and media reporting of this may have victimising effects and may further compound the harms and victimisation that has been or is already being experienced. In the case of health and social care professionals and self-inflicted deaths constructing professionals as 'folk devils' serves to 'other' them and to deny them recognition of the pain and suffering of the loss/death of a service user. It also invisibilises the harmful aftermath in which professionals have to witness, manage and cope with the pains and victimisation of the bereaved.

Caring for, treating and supervising service users or patients who take their own lives is personally and professionally challenging especially in a context which is usually dictated by two converging paradigms – one of care, therapy and rehabilitation and one of control, security and risk management (Taylor, Corteen, & Morley 2014). Visceral reactions exacerbated by the coronial process and media reporting can mean that such complex and difficult realities are ignored or simplified. The impact of the coronial process and media reporting on health and social care professionals who have committed misfeasance requires further critical research to assess the level of victimising effects, as does the manner in which occupations observe and manage this. Another powerful argument for critical empirical investigation in this area is that this is potentially just the beginning of what can be a number of drawn out internal and external, private and public inquiries and litigations for professionals whether they have made a 'mistake' or not.

In relation to the health and social care profession and other occupations that are involved in the care, treatment and/or supervision of service users and involved in self-inflicted deaths, there are other forms of harm and vicitimisation to be considered through a victimological lens.

There "is a cost to caring" (Figley, 1995, p. 1) and professionals may be subjected to the negative effects associated with caring *about* and caring *for* others. In particular those exposed to self-inflicted harms experience vicarious trauma (Gitlin, 1999). Given this and the context of our discussion of occupational communities it is only fitting that we now focus upon the final concept in the victim and victimisation hierarchy, that of tertiary victimisation.

Tertiary victims are to some extent intangible and tertiary victimisation is "diffuse and extends to the community at large" (Burgess et al., 2011, p. 67). Tertiary victimisation "includes a wider circle of 'victims' who may have been affected by a particularly shocking event" (Davies, 2011, p. 196). Tertiary victimisation can be observed among health and social care professionals as they are part of an occupational community. VOCAL (2013) recognises that 'nurses and workers in the field' can be classed as tertiary victims as they suffer 'vicarious victimisation'. Second-hand harm may be experienced through the primary and secondary victimisation of service users, their families, friends and colleagues. As has been indicated earlier, dealing with service users who take their own lives is a very real proposition for those working within psychiatry and associated fields. In a comparison, previous literature has established that emergency service workers can become known as 'tertiary victims' as a result of occupational stress and fatigue in the course of their work (Kratcoski & Das, 2003; Spalek, 2006). Similarly, those professions discussed here face similar demands and pressures in managing their emotions when faced with tragedy and events involving the end of human life. Knowing that self-inflicted deaths may be a routine or common aspect of work (Foley & Kelly, 2007) can be considered as victimising in and of itself. As Elias (1985) contends, by the nature of their work, the police are victimised by the role that they are expected to perform (in terms of dealing with critical incidents, etc.). Whilst not experiencing the immediate physical effects of the harmful act itself, workers may become harmed because of their participation in the response to the traumatic event (Rock, 2007). Moreover, the impacts of self-inflicted deaths and the investigatory procedures that follow can be felt widely. The realisation that service-user self-inflicted deaths can become known as an occupational hazard (Chemtob et al., 1989) may leave a profession feeling anxious, a condition that may be considered as vicarious victimisation whereby those who have no actual victimisation experiences themselves become acutely aware of others who have.

Conclusions
Exposure to the death of a service user impacts in a variety of ways and it can be a traumatic and victimising event for those involved. Health and social care professionals must deal with their own internal professional and personal emotions when a service user they care for, treat, and/or supervise takes their own life. They must do so whilst encountering the victimising effects experienced by family, friends, other service users and colleagues. In addition, more often than not, they must do so in a climate in which professional, political and public visceral reactions – real and imagined – can be placed on a continuum. The visceral reaction continuum begins with professional competence being doubted, negative judgements about professional practices being made and publicly aired, together with assumptions of indifference on the part of the professional and their occupation, potentially ending with the apportioning of blame and responsibility and potential blatant public misrepresentations, 'witch-hunting', 'scapegoating' and 'demonisation'.

Pivotal to this is the Coroner's Inquest and the iatrogenic harm it inadvertently causes. Mandatory participation in the coronial process, together with the verdict (especially if it is a narrative verdict) and media reporting, can play a fundamental role in exacerbating and compounding an already traumatic and victimising event. Whilst the Coroner's Inquest and narrative verdicts allow for central issues to be raised and inadequacies in procedures and practices to be illuminated, invariably there will be an impact on those who were responsible for the care, treatment and/or supervision of the deceased. To some extent this is inevitable and in some cases even desirable; however, care must be taken when a private tragedy becomes a public event through the officialdom of the state (Biddle, 2003; Taylor et al., 2013). This is because the Coroner's Inquest and legal procedures can be a source of distress for the family, health and social care professionals and public service workers more widely, in what can already be a distressful and difficult period of victimisation.

When discussing the victimisation of public service workers as a result of the coronial process, verdict and media reporting we make a clear distinction between public service workers whose actions equate to malfeasance in that they comprise of state organisational deviance and human rights violations and those who equate to misfeasance in the form of regretted, unintentional 'mistake(s)' made in their lines of duty. The victimisation of well-intentioned public service workers (as opposed to unprofessional, corrupt and corruptive public service workers) may be hidden or denied as a result of ideologies concerning victimhood and blameworthiness (Taylor et al., 2013). Through a more imaginative victimological lens we seek to illuminate this situation further.

The Coroner's Inquest and Visceral Reactions

In this chapter we have explored the extent to which the victimological concepts of 'primary', 'secondary' and 'tertiary' victimisation can be applied to health and social care professionals and other public service workers who are exposed to, or involved in, the self-inflicted death of a service user in their care, treatment and/or under their supervision. The concepts of primary, secondary and tertiary victims are to some extent unhelpful if employed to locate victims in a first, second and third order. Doing so detracts from the harm experienced and the nature, extent, occupational contexts and complexities of, immediate responses to, and the aftermath of, victimisation. Victimisation is the process of becoming a *victim* and/or being *victimised*. Whilst this can appear to be a trivial and pedantic case of semantics, there is an important distinction to be made here in order to observe and begin to consider, understand and adequately respond to those involved in cases where service users take their own lives. It enables us to make clearly visible the deceased as a primary victim who has been directly harmed and the victim of intrapersonal violence. It results in the problematisation of family and friends and of witnesses including health and social care professionals as *primary victims* of a self-inflicted death of a service user. The distinction does however enable family, friends and professionals to be observed as victims of *primary victimisation* resulting from the initial victimising event – the self-inflicted death of a service user. Health and social care professionals and other public service workers can also be observed as tertiary victims, vicarious victims and, crucially, as secondary and even possibly primary victims of political and public visceral reactions, exacerbated by the coronial inquest, verdict and media reporting. The extent of victimisation and harm caused with regard to the coronial process, the verdict, media reporting and subsequent investigations and litigations requires further critical qualitative investigation.

References

Alexander, D. A., Klein, S., Gray, N. M., Dewar, I. G., & Eagles, J. M. (2000). Suicide by patients: Questionnaire study of its effect on consultant psychiatrists. *British Medical Journal, 320*, 1571–1573.

Barraclough, B. M., & Shepherd, D. M. (1976). Public interest: Private grief. *British Journal of Psychiatry, 129*, 109–113.

Barraclough, B. M., & Shepherd, D. M. (1977). The immediate and enduring effects of the inquest on relatives of suicide. *British Journal of Psychiatry, 131*, 400–404.

Barton, A., Corteen, K., Scott, D., & Whyte, D. (2007). Conclusion: Expanding the criminological imagination. In A. Barton, K. Corteen, D. Scott & D. Whyte (Eds.), *Expanding the criminological imagination: Critical readings in Criminology* (pp. 198–214). Cullompton, United Kingdom: Willan.

Biddle, L. (2003). Public hazards or private tragedies? An exploratory study of the effect of coroner's procedures on those bereaved by suicide. *Social Science and Medicine, 56*, 1033–1045.

Blood, R., Pirkis, J., & Holland, K. (2007). Media reporting of suicide methods – an Australian perspective. *Crisis – The Journal of Crisis Intervention and Suicide Prevention, 28*(1), 64–69.

Burgess, A. W., Regehr, C., & Roberts, A. R. (2011). *Victimology: Theories and applications.* London, United Kingdom: Jones and Bartlett.

Campbell, C., & Fahy, T. (2002). The role of the doctor when a patient commits suicide. *Psychiatric Bulletin, 26*, 44–49.

Chemtob, C., Bauer, G., Hamada, R., Pelowski, S., & Muraoka, M. (1989). Patient suicide: Occupational hazard for psychologists and psychiatrists. *Professional Psychology: Research & Practice, 20*(5), 294–300.

Chiplin, J., Bos, V., Harris, C., & Codye, D. (1998). *Clinical accountability within the mental health sector: The results of a review conducted on behalf of the mental health commission.* Wellington, New Zealand: The Mental Health Commission.

Christie, N. (1986). The ideal victim. In E. A. Fattah (Ed.), *From crime policy to victim policy* (pp. 17–30). London, United Kingdom: Macmillan.

Cohen, S. (2000). *States of denial: Knowing about atrocities and suffering.* Cambridge, United Kingdom: Polity.

Cornock, M. (2011). A legal commentary on negligence. *Paediatric Nursing, 23*(1), 21–22.

Corteen, K., & Corteen, A. (2012). Dying to entertain? The victimization of professional wrestlers in the USA. *International Perspectives in Victimology, 7*(1), 47–53.

Dare, A. J., Andriessen, K. A., Nordentoft, M., Meier, M., Huisman, A., & Pirkis, J. E. (2011). Media awards for responsible reporting of suicide: Experiences from Australia, Belgium and Denmark. *International Journal of Mental Health Systems, 5*(1), 5–15.

Davies, P. (2011). *Gender, crime and victimisation.* London, United Kingdom: Sage.

Deheegher, J. (2008). Suicide of a service member. In B. K. Wiederhold (Ed.), *Lowering suicide risks in returning troops: Wounds of war* (pp. 129–171). Amsterdam: IOS Press.

Dekker, S. (2013). Prosecuting professional mistake: Secondary victimization and a research agenda for criminology. *International Journal of Criminal Justice Sciences, 4*(1), 60–78.

Dewar, I. G., Eagles, J. M., Klein, S., Gray, N., & Alexander, D. A. (2000). Psychiatric trainees' experiences of, and reactions to, patient suicide. *The Psychiatrist, 24,* 20–23.

Donnelly, L. (2013, June 2). NHS negligence claims rise 20 per cent in just one year. *The Telegraph.* Retrieved from http://www.telegraph.co.uk

Elias, R. (1985). Transcending our social reality of victimization: Toward a new victimology of human rights. *Victimology: An International Journal, 10,* 6–25.

Figley, C. R. (1995). Compassion fatigue as secondary traumatic stress disorder: An overview. In C. R. Figley (Ed.), *Compassion fatigue: Coping with secondary traumatic stress disorder in those who treat the traumatized* (pp. 1–20). New York, NY: Brunner/Mazel.

Fisher, B. S., & Lab, S. P. (2010). *Encyclopedia of victimology and crime prevention.* Thousand Oaks, CA: Sage.

Foley, S. R., & Kelly, B. D. (2007). When a patient dies by suicide: Incidence, implications and coping strategies. *Advances in Psychiatric Treatment, 13,* 134–138.

Gitlin, M. J. (1999). A psychiatrist's reaction to patient suicide. *American Journal of Psychiatry, 156,* 1630–1634.

Goldney, R. D. (2001). The media and suicide: A cautionary view. *Crisis, 22*(4), 173–175.

Goodey, J. (2005). *Victims and victimology: Research, policy and practice.* Harlow, United Kingdom: Pearson.

Green, M. A. (1993). Preservation of forensic evidence in the accident and emergency department. *Accident & Emergency Nursing, 1*(1), 3–7.

Green, P., & Ward, T. (2000). State crime, human rights and the limits of criminology. *Social Justice, 27*(1), 101–115.

Gunnell, D., Hawton, K., & Kapur, N. (2011). Coroners' verdicts and suicide statistics in England and Wales, *British Medical Journal, 343,* 1–2.

Hartley-Parkinson, R., & Nolan, S. (2013, April 30). Coroner slams NHS Trust for 'lamentable failures' after two mental health nurses left man alone to hang himself despite seeing noose. *Mail Online*. Retrieved from http://www.dailymail.co.uk

Hawton, K., & Simkin, S. (2003). Helping people bereaved by suicide. *British Medical Journal, 327*, 177–178.

Herman, H., Trauer, T., & Warnock, J. (2002). The roles and relationships of psychiatrists and other service providers in mental health services. *Australian and New Zealand Journal of Psychiatry, 36*, 75–80.

Herman, J. R. (2000). Suicide reporting. Australian Press Council News, 12(3), 1.

Hill, C., & Cook, L. (2011). Narrative verdicts and their impact on mortality statistics in England and Wales. *Office for National Statistics: Health Statistics Quarterly, 49* (Spring), 81–100.

Hillsborough Independent Panel (2012). *Hillsborough: The Report of the Hillsborough Independent Panel.* London: The Stationery Office, HC581. Retrieved from http://hillsborough.independent.gov.uk/repository/report/HIP_report.pdf

Hobbs, P. (2001). Inquiries – High costs, unacceptable side effects and low effectiveness: Time for revision. *Australasian Psychiatry, 9*(2), 156–160.

Huxley-Binns, R. (2008). When is negligence a crime? *British Journal of Nursing, 18*(14), 892-893.

Jennings, C., & Barraclough, B. (1980). Legal and administrative influences on the English suicide rate since 1900. *Psychological Medicine, 10*(3), 407–418.

Jewkes, Y. (2011). *Media and crime.* (2nd ed.). London, United Kingdom: Sage.

Jones, F. A. (1987). Therapists as survivors of client suicide. In E. J. Dunn, J. L. McIntosh & K. Dunne-Maxim (Eds.), *Suicide and its aftermath: Understanding and counselling its survivors* (pp. 126–141). New York, NY: W. W. Norton.

Karmen, A. (2001). *Crime victims: An introduction to victimology.* (4th ed.). Belmont, CA: Wadsworth.

Karmen, A. (2013). *Crime victims: An introduction to victimology.* (8th ed.). Belmont, CA: Wadsworth.

Kratcoski, P. C., & Das, D. K. (2003). Terrorist victimization: Definitions, focus and impact. In D. K. Das & P. C. Kratcoski (Eds.), *Meeting the challenges of global terrorism: Prevention, control and recovery* (pp. 7–29). Oxford, United Kingdom: Lexington Books.

Landeen, J. J. (1988). Patient suicide: Its impact on the therapeutic milieu of the psychiatric unit. *Perspectives in Psychiatric Care, 24*(2), 74–78.

Linke, S., Wojciak, J., & Day, S. (2002). The impact of suicide on community mental health teams: Findings and recommendations. *Psychiatric Bulletin, 26*, 50–52.

McGovern, J., & McDougall, C. (Directors) (1996, December 5). *Hillsborough.* [Television broadcast]. Manchester, United Kingdom: Granada Television.

Midence, K., Gregory, S., & Stanley, R. (1996). The effects of patient suicide on nursing staff. *Journal of Clinical Nursing, 5*, 115–120.

Ministry of Justice (2011). *Coroners statistics 2010: England and Wales – Ministry of Justice Statistics Bulletin.* Retrieved from http://www.justice.gov.uk/downloads/statistics/mojstats/coroners-bulletin-2010.pdf

Mordue, M., Weatherby, M., Weatherby, S., & Pearson, S. (2012). Distribution of litigation claims across a generalised psychiatric patient journey. *The Psychiatrist, 36*(1), 6–10.

Mullen, R., Admiraal, A., & Trevena, J. (2008). Defensive practice in mental health. *The New Zealand Medical Journal, 121*(1286), 85–91.

Onyett, S. (1995). Responsibility and accountability in community mental health teams. *Psychiatric Bulletin, 19,* 281–285.

Pirkis, J., Blood, R. W., Beautrais, A., Burgess, P., & Skehans, J. (2006). Media guidelines on the reporting of suicide. *Crisis, 27*(2), 82–87.

Pirkis, J., Burgess, P., Blood, R. W., & Francis, C. (2007). The newsworthiness of suicide. *Suicide & Life-Threatening Behavior, 37*(3), 278–283.

Quinney, R. (1972). Who is the victim? *Criminology, 10,* 314–323.

Rock, P. (2007). Theoretical perspectives on victimisation. In S. Walklate (Ed.), *Handbook of victims and victimology* (pp. 37–61). Cullompton, United Kingdom: Willan.

Ruben, H. L. (1990). Surviving a suicide in your practice. In S. J. Blumenthal & D. J. Kupfer (Eds.), *Suicide over the life cycle* (pp. 619–636). Washington, DC: American Psychiatric Press.

Rutty, J. E. (2000). Her Majesty's Coroners and Home Office forensic pathologists perception of the nurses' role in the Coroner's enquiry. *International Journal of Nursing Studies, 37*(4), 351–359.

Scott, S. D., Hirschinger, L. E., Cox, K. R., McCoig, M., Brandt, J., & Hall, L. W. (2009). The natural history of recovery for the healthcare provider "second victim" after adverse patient events. *Quality and Safety in Health Care, 18*(5), 325–330.

Scraton, P., Jemphrey, A., & Coleman, S. (1995). *No last rights: The denial of justice and promotion of myth in the aftermath of the Hillsborough disaster.* Liverpool, United Kingdom: Liverpool City Council.

Spalek, B. (2006). *Crime victims: Theory, policy and practice.* Basingstoke, United Kingdom: Palgrave Macmillan.

Stickley, T., & Felton, A. (2006). Promoting recovery through therapeutic risk taking. *Mental Health Practice, 9*(8), 26-30.

Taylor, P., Corteen, K., & Morley, S. (2013). Service user suicides and the coroner's inquests. *Criminal Justice Matters, 92,* 32-33.

Taylor, P., Corteen, K., & Morley, S. (Eds.). (2014). *A companion to criminal justice, mental health and risk.* Bristol, United Kingdom: Policy Press.

Walklate, S. (2007a). *Imagining the victim of crime.* Maidenhead, United Kingdom: Open University Press.

Walklate, S. (Ed.). (2007b). *Handbook of victims and victimology.* Cullompton, United Kingdom: Willan.

Victims of Crime Assistance League (VOCAL). (2013). Why seek support? Retrieved from http://vocalact.webs.com/seeksupport.htm

Yousaf, F., Hawthorne, M., & Sedgwick, P. (2002). Impact of patient suicide on psychiatric trainees. *The Psychiatrist, 26,* 53-55.

CHAPTER 3

SOLDIERS OF 'CHOICE'?

Ross McGarry

Defining the term 'soldier' is not a complex task. *The Concise Oxford Dictionary* describes a 'soldier' as "a person serving in or having served in an army" (Allen, 1991, p. 1157). As Kümmel (2003) notes the characteristics and purposes of a soldier – as a means in themselves – have been liable to change throughout the centuries: from Greek Spartans, feudal knights and mercenaries of past-times, to the conscripted citizen-soldiers and volunteer professionals of modern military organisations. For our purposes in this chapter we are referring to the modern Weberian soldier of the British armed forces, both men and women suggested as being professionals of their trades, only differentiated from civil servants by their occupational commitment to risk their lives (Rasmussen, 2006), but still characterised by the mainstays of resilience (McGarry, Mythen, & Walklate, 2014), self-sufficiency (McGeorge, Hacker Hughes, & Wessley, 2006) and 'military masculinity' (Woodward, 2000). However, throughout this chapter reference is made to the term 'soldier' in a more generic sense, as Rowe (2006) suggests, offering a description pertaining to both men and women serving in all arms of modern militaries (Navy, Army, Air Force and Marines). Nevertheless, regardless of the variety of these depictions, being a soldier is still a job and the military an employer, particularly when 'service' in the military is voluntary. This is made apparent within the modern British Army (2012) where the opportunities of an army 'career' and to 'move up the ranks' are outlined to potential recruits in their online recruitment information:

> If you work hard at your *job* and show skill, you could soon get your first promotion. You'll lead a small team of soldiers and your *job* will be to help set their tasks for the day and check that the *work* is getting done. You'll get a pay rise, too. As your *career* continues, you'll get extra promotions, more responsibilities and more pay rises. (author's emphases)

Although this explanation appears unremarkable it blurs the distinction between soldiering as a 'career' and soldiering as 'service'. When searching for subject matter relative to this economic relationship the literature is quite disparate suggesting that sociology has failed to fully explicate the job of soldiering in the context of work. For example John Hockey (2009) has previously addressed soldiering in relation to the sensory work of infantrymen in the British military. Here he levels critiques at the sociology of work generally having a dearth of research utilising data "from the working body rather than merely *about* it", in addition to noting the limited research existing on the occupation of soldiering (Hockey, 2009, p. 479). He also explains that when research of this type does emerge it is often in relation to the role of women in the military workplace (Hockey, 2009). Previous literature by Chandler, Bryant, and Bunyard (1995) is an exemplar of Hockey's (2009) point, addressing the tensions experienced by the military due to women being recruited into gender-specific 'military occupations' largely designed for male personnel. Other literature has more squarely addressed issues of work and choice by offering an autobiographical and historical exploration of the variety of reasons why soldiers join the military, the choices they make during service, and the difficult decisions they have to make when they choose to leave (see Rumsby, 2007). However, it fails to acknowledge a soldier's grind to produce the military's most common products: legalised violence, hardship, injury and death. Nevertheless, despite its uncritical approach, this type of coverage provides useful indicators with which to begin exploring the issue of 'choice' and soldiering further.

Therefore this chapter will centre on the occupation of soldiering through reflecting upon the opinions of former British soldiers who had served in (or worked for) the British military both in the UK and on numerous operations overseas. We first look to these participants[1] to provide this chapter with a sense of what constitutes 'choice' when joining the British military. Next, the wider context of these choices and the demographic characteristics of military recruits are examined to demonstrate how the 'choice' to join the British military voluntarily is perhaps determined by socio-economic conditions rather than simply free will. Then the deaths and injuries that have occurred to British service personnel during the wars in Afghanistan and Iraq are provided to outline a darker side of choosing to join the British military, and to offer a means of critiquing the ways in which harms experienced by soldiers are understood. In doing so this chapter not only brings into question the commonplace socio-demographics of the British military but also asks some interesting questions for expanding the capacity of sociology in understanding the lived experiences of soldiering, fighting and the harms

---

[1] Participants included a mix of five males and one female aged between 27 and 55 (two of the males were commissioned officers, the rest were non-commissioned officers) with previous service in combat and support roles: those who had served in Iraq (Operation Telic) include participants from the Army (B, D and E) and the Royal Air Force (A and C); in addition to a participant with joint service in the Royal Navy and Royal Marines (F) who served in Northern Ireland and the first Gulf War.

produced by both. As such it is worth taking this as our starting point and opening this chapter with a brief outline of the theoretical framework within which these issues are couched: victimology.

Putting Victimology to Work
As a first step in depicting the lived experiences of military work, it may appear at a cursory glance that victimology has little to offer, however when aiming to explore the military life experiences of others from a qualitative perspective there is much to be gained here. By allowing an appreciation of the 'lifestyle' of vulnerable groups (see Hindelang, Gottfredson, & Garofalo., 1978; Cohen & Felson, 1979) and the ability to ask critical questions of those who are easily understood as being 'victims' (see Mawby & Walklate, 1994) we are empowered to critically question British soldiers' trajectories into the military via 'choice', their 'lifestyle' during service and potential to experience harm by engaging in war. Understood in this way, victimology provides an analytical lens that not only allows us to question the 'choices' of those who join, but also the consequences of what happens to soldiers during their service. However, before delving into this any further we need to hear what British soldiers have to say about the 'choices' they made upon joining the British armed forces.

Military Service as a 'Choice' of Work
For all participants, military service was cut through with a range of 'choices'. As participant C reflects on a military career which ended in her being medically discharged due to an injury sustained in Iraq:

> I had an element of choice, I chose to join the military, I chose to volunteer for overseas service. ... when I got to Iraq

and I was asked to perform top cover, I could have at that point refused, I would have been returned to unit under a disciplinary procedure, but I still had that choice, it was a choice, it was my choice to get into the back [of the Snatch Land Rover] ... I made the choice that I thought would be good for my career.

Much like Rumsby's (2007) depiction of soldiers of the Victorian army, such 'choices' in these circumstances appear to be both varied and determined by the free will of those doing the 'choosing': from the choice to join the British military, the choice to volunteer for operational service, and the choice to conduct particular duties during conflict. But the issue of choice is more complex than it first presents itself here, not least because military life has disciplinary ramifications for disobeying orders. So in an effort to explicate the work of soldiering further it is worth unpacking some of the participants' reasons for joining the British armed forces as the first 'choice' in pursuing a military career.

Reasons for Joining: Self
Service in the British armed forces is open to members of all socio-economic classes who fit the requisite entry requirements. These are largely based on physical ability, successful achievement of entrance tests and nationality. Minimum age limits apply to applicants (16 years with parental approval, although applications are accepted from as young as 15 years and 7 months); the British Army cadet force is encouraged to keep the interest of those who wish to join, but are younger than the minimum age limits.[2] Nevertheless, participant E explains that many people have 'honourable reasons' for joining the British armed forces. For some

---

[2] See: http://www.army.mod.uk/join/20193.aspx for details.

participants (A, B and F) these 'honourable reasons' were partly based on family influences to join the RAF, army and navy (respectively), they state:

> When I joined the air force my step-father was ex-air force as well so I'd been told quite a bit about it.

> The idea when I was a kid was to join the RAF ... my uncle was a pilot, sort of ended up as a wing commander or a squadron leader or something like that ... started thinking about the army ... my uncle being of that era, so a child in the thirties, [imitates exaggerated high-brow voice] 'well, you've got to join the [UK army regiment] then', you know you've got to join a good regiment, and a good regiment, the best regiment to him from that era was the [UK army regiment], so I started looking at that.

> With a father who had served in Navy Blue I opted for the Royal Navy.

Here it is worth noting that at the point of joining the British armed forces all participants were recruited as non-commissioned ranks, and several (participants A, D and F) shared similar reasons for joining based on their personal pasts, and socio-economic backgrounds. Participant A states his reasons for joining the RAF as a reinvention of his character:

> I wasn't exactly the model child before I joined the military put it that way, so err no it was, it was, it was a good ... it was good to focus me into being a better person if you like.

Whereas participant D joined the army to open up his employment opportunities:

> I wasn't getting any jobs I wasn't doing anything really worthwhile and it was an opportunity ... just thought well, I'm not gunna work in a chip shop for the rest of me life and it was an opportunity to start afresh, be someone anonymous and rebuild my life ... reinvent myself ... I needed something to do and it looked like the best opportunity and I could do something with it.

And participant F reasons his enlistment in the navy as a whim motivated by a lack of success in his younger years:

> I think the motivation for joining the forces anyway came from a period of failed academics at school, determination to become a professional footballer and very quickly got injured out of the game, and walking down to catch the bus back to my home passed the Naval recruiting office, so on a whim, stepped in there ... So motivation for joining, I think failure in everything else.

Reasons for Joining: Others

Participants E and F both had experiences of working directly with the British veteran community in support roles; each provided an insight into why they consider it to be that other people join the British military. For participant F, his perceptions of why others join the British armed forces is a mix of optimism, pessimism, and uncertainty:

> Some of them [British soldiers] are really quite intelligent and just wanna join up for the adventure and the travel.

> I think maybe in the economics we have at the moment, probably find the young nineteen year old squaddy sort of joins because he doesn't want to hang around the streets.

> Some of them are ... perhaps a little less intelligent and think 'well it's the only thing we can do'.

> I think there are a series of reasons but I, you know, difficult to drill down to say, 'well you know we recruit from here because it's a poor area', I don't think that's necessarily the case.

Whereas participant E explains that choices made in civilian life may factor into more 'complicated' and less noble rationales for why some people might join the British military, suggesting:

> [P]ossible that they're victims of their own choices earlier in life ... a lot of people that join the forces ... are often damaged goods when they come in.

> [T]hey [soldiers] join the forces not for Queen and Country, not to provide for their families – well sometimes to provide for their families – but often just to get away from something hurtful and damaging and abusive in their upbringing, to get away from a dad that beats mum up or a dad that beats them up, or some from some sexual abuse, or from inevitable deprivation if they stayed in their home town and therefore their attitude to life doesn't necessarily stand them in good stead for tolerating stresses and strains afterwards, and they're not necessarily the best people to send to war, regardless of what training you can offer them, so the, the army's selection and recruitment and training process ... might have some part to play in that so they could be victim of that, blimey that's complicated.

From both the personal accounts of the participants and their perceptions of others it is possible to deduce that for some the reasons for joining the British military involve a complex network of social factors, including: personal change for the better; employment/career opportunities; a lack of education; adventure and travel; a lack of options in civilian employment; a lack of academic ability; providing for a family; escaping an abusive upbringing; and avoidance of deprivation in civilian life. Now having evidenced some of these 'choices' it is time to start thinking about them in more critically informed ways.

Bringing 'Choice' into Question
The reasons given by Participants (A, B, C, D and F) for joining the British military initially help to bring into question the concept of 'choice', particularly in respect to voluntary service. As Kümmel (2003) notes, since the mid-to-late twentieth century, military forces throughout the member and partner countries of the North Atlantic Treaty Organization[3] (NATO) have experienced a change in the make-up of their workforce. From the end of the Second World War the perceived global threats to NATO changed from the invasion of hostile enemies to the iniquity of terrorism; this change in perceived threat was matched by military forces being reorganised from large conscripted armies to small, more professional organisations (Kümmel, 2003). Membership of these organisations, including the British armed forces, is now (mostly) based on employment rather than conscription. This means that service personnel who choose to serve their nation and work in the military do so of their own volition. However, there is a darker side to these 'choices' as the British military is stratified by a dominant and legitimised caste system based on rank whereby non-commissioned officers and soldiers (non- or junior manager types) are subordinate to commissioned officers (general and senior management types). Given that the majority[4] of British armed forces personnel consist of non-commissioned ranks it is alarming to note that:

---

[3] See http://www.nato.int/cps/en/natolive/index.htm
[4] As at 1 April 2011, Officers = 31,830; Other ranks = 154,520 (Defence Analytic Services and Advice, 2011, p. 5, table 1).

> The armed forces draw non-officer recruits mainly from among young people with low educational attainment and living in poor communities. A large proportion join for negative reasons, including the lack of civilian career options (Gee, 2007, p. 15).

These basic observations go some way to back the participants' experiences of choice when joining the British armed forces and urge us to consider the wider demographics of those who join the British military and *why*.

Demographic Characteristics
As the Ministry of Defence (MoD) does not monitor the socio-demographics of their recruits, and without wanting to expose this discussion to a basic two-dimensional stratification at the outset, some inferences about the wider demographic characteristics of the British military have to be made here. First, the workforce of the British military is made up of four dominant categories: white (93.3%), male (90.4%), non-commissioned ranks (82.9%), between the ages of 20[5] and 30[6] (Defence Analytic Services and Advice, 2011). Second, as Gee (2007) and as Gee and Goodman (2010) suggest, the MoD has been shown to pool its recruits from lower socio-economic groups from around the UK, in addition to which 75% of the British military's employment is of young recruits between the ages of (under) 18 and 25[7] into non-commissioned ranks (Defence Analytic Services and Advice, 2011). This is not to suggest that the services of minority ethnic groups, females, older personnel, or those from higher socio-economic backgrounds are rendered invisible in this discussion. But it is

---
[5] 20–24 = 23.1%.
[6] 25–29 = 22.5%.
[7] Under 18 = 27.6%, 18–19 = 22%, 20–24 = 31.9%. Total = 75.6%.

possible to 'deduce and summarise' (as Hindelang et al., 1978 suggested) that the demographic characteristics of young, white males from lower socio-economic groups are largely representative of the majority of recruits entering and serving in the British military. This is of particular interest to victimology given that white, heterosexual males have been the demographic that has traditionally been used as a 'measuring stick' by which to decipher the 'victim' from the 'non-victim' within victimology (Walklate, 2007).

Reasons for Joining
Reporting in 2005 on the educational and socio-economic backgrounds of non-commissioned recruits into the British Army, the Select Committee on Defence (2005) stated that:

> It is a generally accepted truth that the Army recruits most of its soldiers from the lowest socio-economic groups in the country. The status of a soldier, while often admired, has never been high, and joining the Army has always been seen as a good option for young people with few qualifications or difficult pasts. (p. 263, Ev 255)

Both the Select Committee on Defence (2005, p. 263–264, Ev 255–256) and Gee (2007) highlight the findings of a rare study of the socio-economic backgrounds of British Army recruits in Cardiff between 1999 and 2000, which detailed:

- Just over 60% had left school with no academic qualifications.
- 14% had more than five GCSEs at grades A–C.[8]

---

[8] Gee (2007, p. 16) only, this is stated as '70 of the recruits' in The Select Committee on Defence (2005, p. 264, Ev 256).

The Select Committee on Defence (2005) further informed from an internal MoD source that:

> Latest Army research suggests that up to 50% of all recruits joining the Service have literacy or numeracy skills at levels at or below those expected of an 11 year old. (p. 264, Ev 256)

This low attainment is perhaps emblematic of Gee and Goodman's (2010) most recent research highlighting that the British Army has been found to focus more of its recruiting practices in the most disadvantaged schools in London. However, beyond the recruitment of those with low academic attainment the Select Committee on Defence (2005) and Gee (2007, p. 16) further informed on the Cardiff study that of the British soldiers surveyed:

- 69% were found to have come from a broken home.
- 50% were classified as coming from a deprived background.
- 16% had been long term unemployed before joining.
- 35% had had more than eight different jobs since leaving school (nearly all on a casual basis).
- 40% were joining the Army as a last resort.

This lends some weight to the assertion by Wessley (cited in Hansard, 2005, para. 41) that not only do some members of the British armed forces "come from 'somewhat dubious backgrounds'", but that "both the British and American militaries contain an overrepresentation of those from disadvantaged backgrounds and regions of the country" (Wessley, 2005, p. 464; see also Wessley, 2004). Although some of the earlier reasons for joining provided by participant E suggest choices for military enrolment are freely made and hedonistic, others can be understood as "structural constraints" (see Hindelang et al., 1978, p. 242), bound to socio-economic conditions that place limitations on the 'choices' people may have (or make) prior to joining the British armed forces. Taking these socio-economic circumstances into consideration, for those who join the British military this suggests that the question of 'choice', although made freely, may be influenced by other wider socio-demographic issues relating to a soldier's domestic background, education and limited chances of pursuing successful civilian employment.

But of course these observations are nothing new and do perhaps play to some normative assumptions of the social demographics of many British soldiers and the stratification of the British military more broadly. But this in and of itself is a cause for concern. Although the military is vastly populated with young men and women from disadvantaged backgrounds, as this chapter has demonstrated, this is rarely addressed, discussed or – more importantly – critiqued. We can perhaps also assume then that there are other knowledges about British soldiers that are passed over as commonplace in similar ways, without being exposed to critical scrutiny. Typical exemplars of this are injuries and deaths as a result of 'working' for the military.

War at Work: What are the Consequences?
To date more than 500 British service personnel have been killed during the wars in Afghanistan and Iraq. Quantifying the spread of this violence Bird and Fairweather (2007) report that 53% [9] of military deaths in Iraq were caused by im-

---

[9] 493 IED deaths from a total of 973 overall deaths between 1 January 2006 and 4 February 2007.

provised Explosive Devices (IEDs); in addition to 15%[10] of deaths in Afghanistan being caused by IEDs and 10%[11] of deaths by suicide bombings. In addition, further data from iCasualties (2010) show that IED deaths in Afghanistan have progressively increased over the past decade, rising from none in 2001 to 275 in 2009, and accounting for 58%[12] of all military deaths in the country during 2010. There are of course countless more British soldiers who have sustained varying degrees of physical and psychological injury during this period. In the eyes of International Humanitarian Law (IHL) and the constitutions of The Hague Convention such deaths and injuries against British soldiers are defined as being caused by 'illegal tactics'. Moreover when British soldiers are killed by insurgents in Afghanistan or Iraq they are killed by 'unjust' combatants who are effectively using *de jure* prohibited tactics. Taken together this renders British soldiers as victims of violent crime (see Rayment, 2006). However, as Stanley (2009) explains, "the reliance on classifications and figures can be sanitizing, distracting and sometimes harmful" (p. 61) to those suffering from individual or collective harms. This leads us to suggest that the reduction of the deaths and injuries of British soldiers to publicly accessible, quantifiable and measurable data perhaps sanitises the extent and impact of what they experience during the work that they do. Coupling this information with the low socio-economic and disadvantaged backgrounds that the MoD recruits from, and

---

[10] 76 IED deaths from a total of 518 overall deaths between 1 January 2006 and 4 February 2007.
[11] 15 suicide bombing deaths from a total of 157 overall deaths between 1 May 2006 and 4 February 2007.
[12] 293 IED deaths from a total of 412 overall deaths between 1 January 2010 and 24 August 2010.

the majority of those they recruit (white, young males) being both the most likely to experience violent crime as civilians (see Walklate, 2007), and the most likely to be killed in Afghanistan and Iraq (see iCasualties, 2011), it is possible to capture that "[t]he effects of victimization strike particularly hard at the poor, the powerless, the disabled and the socially isolated" (United Nations Office for Drug Control and Crime Prevention, 1999, p. 5).

In the circumstances described above we can perhaps begin to see soldiers fitting comfortably into this definition, offering us a different way of conceptualising death and injury counts at war. By framing British soldiers as frequently being recruited from vulnerable civilian populations and potentially becoming victims of violent crime during war urges the concept of 'choice' to be broadened further still. Here we turn to the thoughts of Robert Elias (1986), who states:

> We cannot overestimate the enormous impact of victimization on people's lives. Yet, as significant as the effects we have described may be, they still understate the overall victimization suffered. We will suggest that we cannot appreciate the true burden of victimization until we employ broader indicators of victimization that transcend our narrow criminal definition. In other words, we should consider applying more universal standards of human rights. (p. 131)

Earlier in this chapter a brief debate has been raised in relation to the legal rights and protections of British soldiers serving in Afghanistan and Iraq and urged a rethink of how they should be re-imagined as workers and the British military as their employer (McGarry, 2012). Within this framework is an outline of how British soldiers should be conceived as being held in a 'state of exception' (Agamben, 2005) when killed or injured during the wars in Afghanistan and Iraq due to the MoD not being accountable as employers for their deaths and injuries within either health and safety or human rights legislations. Elsewhere I have provided more detailed attention to concerns regarding British soldiers' right to life in relation to how they have been poorly equipped and trained for serving in Afghanistan and Iraq (McGarry, Mythen, & Walklate, 2012). The suggestion here is that not only have British soldiers been held in a state of exception, but there are also techniques of neutralisation (Sykes & Matza, 1957) and forms of denial (Cohen, 2001) at work on behalf of the State in failing to accept responsibility for the protection of soldiers' well-being, masked behind the notion of 'unlimited liability' and the Military Covenant. A recent landmark case heard in the Court of Appeal offered this position some additional legal credibility whereby the families of several soldiers killed in Iraq won a long battle to hold the MoD to account for the deaths of their children due to them being inadequately protected when working for the British armed forces at war (Meikle, 2012). The comments of Susan Smith (cited in ITN, 2012), the mother of Private Phillip Hewett who was killed in Iraq whilst travelling in a Snatch Land Rover in 2005, captures the essence of these arguments:

> This is a case of an employer owing his staff the right duty of care, take away the uniform and everything else, it's simply a man or a woman doing their job, and they should be respected for doing that job the same as anybody else.

By observing the economic relationship of her son, a soldier, to his employer, the military, these comments squarely address soldiering as work and the normalised inequalities that are inherent within this type of employment. Following a further ruling from the Supreme Court in June 2013 the MoD is now fully accountable as an employer to provide a duty of care to soldiers serving on operations (not just on military bases overseas) with respect to their right to life (*BBC News*, 2013). However, whereas before soldiering and the harms that come with it have been held in exception by the State (McGarry & Walklate, 2011; McGarry et al., 2012), the plight of Susan Smith and other bereaved families of service personnel has slowly begun to illuminate upon, and formally address, the imbalance experienced by British soldiers who 'choose' to join the British armed forces and face unnecessary danger as a consequence of their work.

Conclusions
As a concluding note we can critically reflect upon the words of the late British military historian John Fortescue (1934) who states:

> The British soldier, supposed to represent physical force only, is a great moral force within and without the Empire. It is not with physical weapons only, nor even chiefly, that he contends all the world over for the honour, in the highest sense, of his Regiment, of the Army and of the Nation. And he prevails because he makes some conscience of what he does. He knows what he is fighting for and loves what he knows. (pp. 7–8)

This explanation depicts British soldiers as dutiful and serving for national honour and Empire. Moreover this description suggests a British soldier who is well informed and, perhaps, afforded enough agency to do a job that they love: fighting. However this sentiment is clearly dated, and in light of our discussion presents itself as out of touch with the modern British military. However, they do connect with the arguments made throughout this chapter, in particular how much military recruits know about the work they are going to be engaging in when they 'choose' to join the military. As Gee (2007) explains, new recruits into the British armed forces are largely ill-informed of the dangers they may face and are perhaps unaware of their commitment to the 'unlimited liability' they are privy to, or the tenets of the military covenant to which they subscribe. As such:

> Recruitment literature for the army glamorises warfare, poorly explains the terms of service and largely omits to mention the risks of the career. It is common for recruits to enlist without knowing the risks or their legal rights and obligations (Gee, 2007, p. 1).

So the nostalgia of moral force, national honour, and knowledge of what is being fought for and at what costs – as outlined by Fortescue (1934) – are easily destabilised when squared with basic sociological notions of choice, class and work.

However, this approach also requires more to be demanded of it. If conceiving of military employees who legally brandish violence under the jurisdiction of the State as being vulnerable, then we must also turn this analysis outwards to draw other vulnerable groups into similar discussions. This not only includes the (literally) countless numbers of civilians killed in the wars in Afghanistan and Iraq, but also those who the British military are 'fighting' against. In a similar way to young people from disadvantaged backgrounds joining the British military, so too must we consider those who are manipulated into joining extremist organisations, insurgencies, paramilitaries and other disenfranchised groups. It is not a huge leap of the imagination to consider that those who end up exerting violence on one another – on behalf of more powerful benefactors (political, religious or otherwise) – may well have similar socio-demographic characteristics. As Hindelang et al. (1978) suggest, "it is time to move beyond the data" (p. 241) and begin to develop more sophisticated understandings of the 'choices' people make not only working in the military, but also going to, and being at, war.

References
Agamben, G. (2005). *State of exception*. Chicago, IL: University of Chicago Press.
Allen, R. E. (Ed.). (1991). *Concise Oxford dictionary*. London, United Kingdom: BCA.
BBC News. (2013). Iraq damages cases: Supreme Court rules families can sue. Retrieved from http://www.bbc.co.uk/news/uk-22967853
Bird, S. M., & Fairweather, C. B. (2007). Military fatality rates (by cause) in Afghanistan and Iraq: a measure of hostilities. *International Journal of Epidemiology, 36*, 841–846.
British Army. (2012). Soldier careers. Retrieved from http://www.army.mod.uk/join/20197.aspx
Chandler, J., Bryant, L., & Bunyard, L. (1995). Notes and issues: Women in military occupations. *Work, Employment & Society, 9*(1), 123–135.
Cohen, S. (2001). *States of denial: Knowing about atrocities and suffering*. Cambridge, United Kingdom: Polity.
Cohen, L. E., & Felson, M. (1979). Social change and crime pattern trends: A routine activity approach. *American Sociological Review, 44*, 588–608.
Defence Analytic Services and Advice. (2011). *United Kingdom Defence Statistics 2011*. Retrieved from http://www.dasa.mod.uk/modintranet/UKDS/UKDS2011/pdf/c/ukds.pdf

Elias, R. (1986). *The politics of victimization: Victims, victimology and human rights*. Oxford, United Kingdom: Oxford University Press.

Fortescue, J. (1934). *The last post*. London, United Kingdom: W. M. Blackwood & Sons.

Gee, D. (2007). Informed choice? Armed forces recruitment practice in the United Kingdom. Retrieved from http://www.informedchoice.org.uk/informedchoice/informed choicefull.pdf

Gee, D., & Goodman, A. (2010). Army recruiters visit London's poorest schools most often. Retrieved from http://www.informedchoice.org.uk/armyvisitstoschools.pdf

Hansard. (2005). Recruitment. Retrieved from http://www.publications.parliament.uk/pa/cm200405/cmselect/cmdfence/63/6306.htm

Hindelang, M. J., Gottfredson, M. R., & Garofalo, J. (1978). *Victims of personal crime: An empirical foundation for a theory of personal victimization*. Cambridge, MA: Ballinger Publishing.

Hockey, J. (2009). 'Switch on': Sensory work in the infantry. *Work, Employment & Society, 23*(3), 477–493.

iCasualties.org. (2011). Operation Iraqi Freedom. Retrieved from http://icasualties.org/Iraq/IraqiDeaths.aspx

ITN. (2012). Defence: Families of soldiers killed fighting in Iraq win right to sue MoD for negligence: High court statements. Retrieved from http://www.itnsource.com

Kümmel, G. (2003). A soldier is a soldier is a soldier!? The military and its soldiers in an era of globalization. In G. Caforio (Ed.), *Handbook of the sociology of the military* (pp. 417–433). New York, NY: Springer.

Mawby, R. I., & Walklate, S. (1994). *Critical victimology: International perspectives*. London, United Kingdom: Sage.

McGarry, R. (2012). The workplace of war: Unlimited liability or safety crimes? *Criminal Justice Matters, 89*(1), 6–7.

McGarry, R., & Walklate, S. (2011). The soldier as victim: Peering through the looking glass. *British Journal of Criminology, 51*(6), 900–917.

McGarry, R., Mythen, G., & Walklate, S. (2012). The soldier, human rights and the military covenant: A permissible state of exception? *International Journal of Human Rights: Special Issue, 16*(8), 1183–1195.

McGarry, R., Walklate, S., & Mythen, G. (2014). A sociological analysis of military resilience: Opening up the debate. *Armed Forces & Society.* OnlineFirst. doi: 10.1177/0095327X13513452

McGeorge, T., Hacker Hughes, J., & Wessley, S. (2006). The MoD PTSD decision: A psychiatric perspective. *Occupational Health Review, 122,* 21–28.

Meikle, J. (2012). Relatives of UK soldiers killed in Iraq win right to seek compensation. Retrieved from http://www.guardian.co.uk/uk/2012/oct/19/relatives-soldiers-iraq-damages-claims

Rasmussen, M. V. (2006). *The risk society at war.* Cambridge, United Kingdom: Cambridge University Press.

Rayment, S. (2006, December 10). Wounded troops to get millions in compensation. *The Sunday Telegraph.* (p. 1).

Rowe, P. J. (2006). *The impact of human rights law on armed forces.* Cambridge, United Kingdom: Cambridge University Press.

Rumsby, J. H. (2007). Making choices: Constructing a career in the ranks of the early Victorian army. *The Society for Army Historical Research: Special Publication, 16,* 23–33.

Select Committee on Defence. (2005). *Duty of care: Third report of session 2004–05: Volume II.* London, United Kingdom: The Stationery Office. Retrieved from http://www.

publications.parliament.uk/pa/cm200405/cmselect/cmdfence/63/63ii.pdf

Stanley, E. (2009). *Torture, truth and justice: The case of Timor-Leste*. Abingdon, United Kingdom: Routledge.

Sykes, G. M., & Matza, D. (1957). Techniques of neutralization: A theory of delinquency. *American Sociological Review, 22*(6), 664–670.

United Nations Office for Drug Control and Crime Prevention (1999). *Handbook on justice for victims: On the use and application of the declaration of basic principles of justice for victims of crime and abuses of power within their criminal justice systems*. Retrieved from http://www.uncjin.org/Standards/9857854.pdf

Walklate, S. (2007). *Imagining the victim of crime*. Maidenhead, United Kingdom: Open University Press.

Wessley, S. (2004). Risk, psychiatry and the military. *Annual Liddell Hart Centre for Military Archives Lecture*. Retrieved from http://www.kcl.ac.uk/lhcma/info/lec04.shtml

Wessley, S. (2005). Risk, psychiatry and the military. *British Journal of Psychiatry, 186*, 459–466.

Woodward, R. (2000). Warrior heroes and little green men: Soldiers, military training, and the construction of rural masculinities. *Rural Sociology, 65*(4), 640–657.

CHAPTER 4

WORKING-CLASS GAMBLING ENTREPRENEURS

Carolyn Downs

In a chapter that explores entrepreneurial activity amongst the working classes in Britain over a time period of around 200 years, it seems appropriate to take as a starting definition of 'entrepreneurship' one that was developed during the great mercantile expansion of the mid-eighteenth century. Richard Cantillon (1755) coined the term 'entrepreneur' to represent that group of people who gained their income neither from inherited land nor from wage labour. He separated out entrepreneurship from other types of economic activity on the basis that uncertainty was the central characteristic of entrepreneurial behaviour and activities, in contrast for example, with holding land, which offered a more certain economic return. The central point for Cantillon: that entrepreneurship was a consequence of generating an economic return in a situation where the individual engaged in the activity will pay a certain price following that of the place where they purchase it, to resell wholesale or retail at an uncertain price (Cantillon, 1755, p. i.xiii). Cantillon further asserted that an entrepreneur was dealing with known costs (in this case the odds) and unknown demand and in doing so brought stability to markets by correctly anticipating consumer preferences (Cantillon, 1755, p. i.xiii). J. S. Mill (1848) later agreed that entrepreneurs were characterised by the need to bear risks as well as to manage their business; this definition is useful when considering the development of gambling entrepreneurship. This chapter will show how the risks of imprisonment were set against the need to attract customers, otherwise known as punters. Schumpeter (1954) stressed innovation as important in defining entrepreneurship; gambling entrepreneurs have had to continuously innovate to stay ahead of the law. Liles (1974) noted that becoming an entrepreneur was itself putting at risk personal financial stability, personal relationships, career progression and psychological well-being, a definition that is perhaps less useful here, although a proportion of entrepreneurs of gambling were imprisoned or fined. Hisrich and Brush (1985) generated a definition of entrepreneurship that explicitly recognised elements of risk, stating that entrepreneurship required "assuming the accompanying financial, psychic and social risks, and receiving the resulting rewards of monetary and personal satisfaction" (p. 15). Risk, is therefore, one of the defining features of entrepreneurship.

The 200 years under consideration here cover a time period in which the initial acceptance of gambling as part of everyday life in post-Restoration and eighteenth-century Britain, was replaced first by attempts to limit the gambling of the masses through piecemeal legislation, and then with the legalisation and regulation of commercial gambling. Over that period the working-class entrepreneurs organised commercial gambling for the masses, only to lose out in 1961 to large leisure corporations such as Mecca (Downs, 2010). In post-Restoration Britain gambling was almost ubiquitous, to the distress of some social commentators such as the eminent jurist William Blackstone (1723–1780) who commented:

> It [gambling] is an offence of the most alarming nature; tending by necessary consequence to promote public idleness, theft and debauchery among those of a lower class; and among persons of a superior rank, it has frequently been attended with the sudden ruin and desolation of ancient and

opulent families, an abandoned prostitution of every principle of honour and virtue. (Cited in Milsom, 1981, p. 83)

Indeed, the provision of opportunities to gamble required the codification of sports such as boxing, cricket and pedestrianism (Radford, 2001) and encouraging the wider development of horse racing (Huggins, 2000) as well as supporting the development of clubs for gentlemen and hells for the hoi polloi. However, the birth of evangelical Christianity towards the end of the eighteenth century, the rise of the movement for rational recreation, increased levels of social control as a result of the industrial revolution and the determination of social reformers to protect the working classes from themselves (Thompson, 1961) led to a series of legislative changes that restricted the opportunities for gambling and left gambling entrepreneurship in the black economy. The outcome of a gamble is always uncertain but this chapter will argue that gambling entrepreneurship in fact offered a fairly certain return for manageable levels of risk and this made it an attractive, if generally illegal option, for the working classes in general and often provided a regular income for poorer women.

Gambling and Entrepreneurship
There have almost certainly been entrepreneurs of gambling as long as gambling has existed. Commercial gambling was prevalent throughout the Roman Empire, with taverns alongside Roman roads offering a range of dice-based games, as well as early forms of bingo. Gambling was recognised as a widespread social problem and laws were passed restricting it; an unusual step for the Romans to take as the state did not generally interfere with business activities or private behaviour (Kowalski, 2000; Milani-Santarpia, 2011). However,

rules on gambling for money and in public were easily circumvented by operators issuing tokens or chips for play and through gaming moving into private clubs. These are the same tactics adopted by gambling entrepreneurs throughout the period under discussion here as they innovated to keep slightly ahead of the laws designed to restrict or prevent gambling in Britain.

Gambling is widely viewed as more of a vice or minor social aberration than legitimate leisure or business opportunity. The legal status between the Restoration of 1660 and 1960 when most types of gambling were legalised was broadly one of attempted control, prohibition or restriction, with nevertheless significant amounts of gambling taking place and much gambling being effectively run for commercial profit (Ashton, 1898; Clark, 1983; Clapson, 1991). Gambling is an ideal vehicle for enterprise. People like to gamble, ensuring a ready supply of customers; stakes can be small, widening the customer base; the way that most gambling games work ensures that the profit lies with the provider of the gambling service and even with games of skill the use of table fees ensures there is a profit for the organiser, who is also usually the dealer and thus gains house advantage. Whilst there is an assumption of gambling as the activity of men, in fact, whenever there are studies, rates of gambling between the genders are generally similar (Kemsley & Ginsburg, 1951) and it was probably always a cross-gender activity, a finding reflected amongst the existence of women entrepreneurs of gambling prior to the legalisation of the activity in 1960.

Studies of entrepreneurship even as recently as the 1980s have concluded that women are generally significantly less likely to be entrepreneurs and it has been thought that, historically, entrepreneurial activity amongst women was extremely limited (Birley, 1988). In fact, it may be the case not

Working-Class Gambling Entrepreneurs

so much that women were not finding opportunities to be entrepreneurial but rather that they have been entrepreneurial in areas of endeavour such as the domestic sphere where their efforts have not been documented (Bradley, 1989). There has also been considerable debate about whether female entrepreneurs are different to male, or different to non-entrepreneurial women (Birley, 1988; DeMartino & Barbato, 2003) with studies finding little difference in psychological characteristics but noting that the motivations of women can be different to those of men (Birley, 1988). Certainly, almost all gambling entrepreneurs, male or female, were working in the black economy until 1961, but records are limited and dispersed. While it is well known that men were organising commercial gambling, often associated with sporting activities such as boxing, pedestrianism or football (Clapson, 1991; Chinn, 1991; Radford, 2001) women from all classes and all historical periods saw the commercial potential of gambling too, and used it as a means of earning an income (Dawson, 1962; Roberts 1984, 1995, Downs, 2009). Women publicans provided opportunities for customers to gamble (Clark, 1983; Kirkby, 1997; Wright, 2001). Upper-class women organised gambling parties with 'card money' being paid to the hostess, women were organising bingo (also known as tombola, house or lotto) after the First World War, and lotteries and sweepstakes from at least 1700 and probably earlier (Downs, 2009). Women provided racing tips, were legal credit bookmakers (Dawson, 1962 and illegal cash bookmakers (Roberts, 1984, 1995; Chinn, 1991), acted as bookies' runners (Beckwith, 1971) and were unofficial agents for the Irish Hospitals Sweepstake which was illegal in England, Scotland, Wales and Northern Ireland (Coleman, 2005). Running illegal gambling games provided a route out of poverty for both men and women prior to 1961. There is evidence in court papers, parliamentary inquiries, press, diaries (such as that of Horace Walpole), charitable organisation minutes and other sources that throughout the 300 years between the Restoration and legalisation of gambling that women, and mainly working-class women, were significantly involved in developing opportunities to make money out of the desire of others to gamble. This was perhaps because it offered a safer and better-remunerated means of earning a living than other options such as taking in laundry (respectable but hard work and poorly paid), prostitution (illegal, dangerous and a sure route to social ostracism) or working as a live-in servant (difficult if you had caring responsibilities), or it could have been that women who wanted to gamble preferred games organised by a woman. While gambling was often illegal it was also a normal part of life for the great majority of working people so that the women and men who provided gambling services seem to have been respected members of their local communities who had a degree of agency in their lives granted by the money they earned through the gambling of others.

Gambling and the Social Role of Money
One issue around attitudes towards gambling, and perhaps also part of an unspoken rationale for the social control of gambling, appears to be the related issue of the social importance of money. Western capitalism has developed through the use of money as a means of exchange, and since industrialisation money has become one of the basic building blocks of Western society (Cross, 1993; Sonnenberg, 2008). Without access to money it is difficult for people to live in Western society. This fact has given money a power and identity that in pre-industrial societies, where land was far more important to survival than money, it did not have. As

society increasingly moved towards a market economy so money, as the primary means of exchange, gained increased social significance (Cross, 1993). This in turn encouraged a discourse around the proper use of money with notions such as fecklessness, improvidence and poverty seen as social ills leading to unrest, while thrift, saving and investment were the primary means of self and societal improvement (Bailey, 1987).

In a social system where money has power and identity, possession of money carries with it responsibility; however, gambling implies a lack of care for money, along with the opportunity to gain money without effort. In a capitalist society neither of these options buttresses the social system; indeed, they might be seen as in direct opposition to the social system. That capitalism itself is predicated upon risk-taking and gambling is an uncomfortable truth, and one that causes such difficulties that society has developed a whole raft of techniques to disguise the similarities between the two. So although the earliest forms of life insurance (tontines) were seen as gambles, with the prospectus for a 1674 tontine in London asking: "What is the hazard of losing £20 in comparison to the great advantage that may be obtained by survivorship?" (Kopf, 1927, p. 254), the notion that insurance was a commercial transaction became quickly established and the link with gambling was rapidly seen as undesirable. As the early financial institutions developed it became very much in the interests of establishments such as Lloyds of London to ensure that the activities they were engaged in were not viewed as gambling. In the case of Lloyds of London this included developing a physical separation. The coffee house where business had been conducted from 1688 became so closely identified with the gambling games played by significant numbers of patrons that in 1770, the members of Lloyds decided that a substantial geographical distance must be established in order to maintain the integrity of their risk-related, highly speculative business (Kopf, 1927). A further separation of commercial speculation from gambling resulted from the development of a specialist language that allowed ideas about risk linked to money to be codified. In this context, a premium is paid or an investment made rather than a bet being laid and dividends are earned rather than winnings collected by investors smart enough to have followed the market and predicted its course (Downs, 2009). The same technique was successfully adopted by John Moores with Littlewoods pools paying a dividend and not issuing winnings and encouraging players to use their skill and knowledge of the game of football to invest in the pools rather than recklessly placing a bet. Gambling, as opposed to investment and speculation, is clearly identified as the reverse of thrift. The idea that money could be acquired without effort, that decisions about how money was spent could be made on the basis of random numbers or superstitions, that people could achieve a transformation of their lives through an activity that represented a lack of care for something as important as money was anathema to many people. The difference in attitudes between those with power and money who were free to speculate or gamble as they chose and the powerless labouring-class gambler became, in the centuries after the Restoration period, a key battleground for control of society.

Poverty and Risk
The poorest people have always lived the riskiest lives. They tend to have jobs with higher rates of accidents and deaths, their housing tenure is often not secure, they have little agency in their work, in their life choices or in the places where they live. One finding that continues to puzzle researchers is that

although the largest group of non-gamblers is found among the poorest groups in society, nevertheless 61% of this group gamble regularly (Wardle, 2007). The poorest people appear to spend relatively small amounts regularly (which nevertheless are often significant proportions of their income) on an activity that can be regarded as irrational. This paradox has been noted in the past. Lady Florence Bell (1907), B. S. Rowntree (1901, 1941) and Ferdynand Zweig (1948, 1952, 1961) all commented on the same apparently irrational behaviour and proposed a range of explanations for the persistence of gambling including the desire to get something for nothing (Rowntree, 1901), the fact that people like them did win through gambling (Bell, 1907) and that gambling was their hobby (Zweig, 1952). Indeed, George Orwell (1937) commented on the prevalence of gambling amongst poor people and concluded that it provided, "the cheapest of all luxuries. Even people on the verge of starvation can buy a few days hope ('Something to live for', as they call it) by having a penny on a sweepstake" (Orwell, 1937, p. 80). More recently in studies funded by the Joseph Rowntree Foundation, "Most people on low incomes dream of winning the pools or the National Lottery" (Kempson, 1996, p. 8) with Emma Casey (2003) noting poor women in her study of lottery play "were motivated by the prizes that they occasionally won" (p. 253), and that daydreams about winning were important in the daily lives of her study cohort. One of the unseen consequences of poverty is the impact it can have on individuals' will to act, with Myers (2000) explaining that "[s]evere poverty demoralises people when it erodes their sense of control" (p. 329). While there is evidence that gambling acts provide hope of escape from poverty, which perhaps accounts for the prevalence of gambling amongst poorer people, providing gambling opportunities for others appears to have provided a regular income for those in the working classes who became gambling entrepreneurs. They established a means of earning a crust (and often a comfortable living) through organising gambling opportunities in their communities and they provided the hope others needed through recognising that it was a saleable commodity within their community. These gambling opportunities ranged from small-scale gambling games for fewer than ten people to larger-scale events attracting several hundreds.

The Role of Capital and Labour in Facilitating Gambling Entrepreneurship
The move of masses of people into the cities and towns in the post-Restoration period assisted in the expansion of opportunities for organising gambling games on a commercial basis. Unlike traditional forms of investment-based business venturing during this period (which required access to capital in order to start up), gambling ventures needed nothing more than a notepad and pencil, knowledge of the game and a degree of confidence in one's ability to run the game so as to ensure punters had sufficient confidence in the organiser to pay and play. Thus gambling entrepreneurship undermines conventional societal expectations of capital, and therefore externally verified markers of social responsibility, such as saving or being considered credit-worthy as a pre-requisite for business. Furthermore, as gambling was largely an illegal activity before 1961 many entrepreneurs of gambling were operating in the black economy. Some certainly provided opportunities for money laundering, there were turf wars, murders took place, officers of the law were bribed and little, if any, tax was paid (Chinn, 1991; Clapson, 1991; Downs, 2009).

Working-Class Gambling Entrepreneurs

Initially the post-Restoration government itself initiated an annual gambling event, the State Lottery, to help with raising funds for public projects. By 1694 the popularity of these lotteries was such that one million pounds was raised by the State Lottery of that year (Ashton, 1898, p. 227). The scale of spending on the lottery gives an idea of the capacity of the lottery as a means of raising revenue, as well as of the willingness of the people to gamble. Tickets were ten guineas each, so this was not designed to be a gambling opportunity poor people could access, but in fact poorer people were not barred from lottery play by price; they would form a syndicate to purchase a ticket or take part in the many smaller private lotteries which had tickets at one penny, or they would bet on the lottery draw itself. In 1721 all private lotteries were banned, although the ban was largely ineffective and they appear to have remained very popular with the poor. Given the complete lack of a nationally effective law enforcement infrastructure at this time, such commercially profitable gambling games were impossible to prevent; they had small stakes and were easy to play, plus there was the potential for a large prize if enough people were taking part. These illegitimate lotteries were colloquially known as 'Little Goes', and despite intermittent prosecutions of those running them they flourished throughout the country. They varied from penny lotteries run in the slums or poorer quarters of towns to the private disposals of goods by the wealthy, and are likely to have attracted players from all levels of society (Ashton, 1898; Clark, 1983).

All accounts of lotteries, including evidence given to two Select Committees established by the House of Commons, indicate that a large percentage of tickets were purchased by women, and that women often organised both the illegal lotteries and lottery insurances that were important parts of gambling culture of the period up to 1826. However, women were not only organising lotteries, they were running gambling houses in premises as varied as upper-class salons to working-class taverns (Ashton, 1898; Clark, 1983; Russell, 2000). The spread of specialised premises at which gambling was the primary purpose also appears to have provided public venues where women could gamble on card or dice games (Russell, 2000). By the 1720s there were at least 30 public gaming houses in Covent Garden alone, with many more across London and throughout smaller provincial cities (Clark, 1983). There was an increasing outpouring of public anxiety about the sharp practices that ensued in such places, articulated by *The Grub Street Journal* of 2 September 1739:

> These societies consist mostly of two or three insignificant old Maids, the same number of gay widows, a batter'd old Beau or two ... In these places it is that young ladies of moderate fortunes are drawn in ... and when by false cards, slipping, signs and crimp, they are stript of their last Guinea, their wretched companions will not know them.

While high stake, high society gambling was widely reported; gambling was prevalent across all levels of society. Gillian Russell (2000) commented that the willingness of the aristocracy, especially well-born women, in commercialising gambling "demonstrated the adaptability of the British aristocracy at this period [late eighteenth century] ... in its embracing of the possibilities of the commercialisation of culture" (p. 488). However, gambling entrepreneurship was not left to the aristocracy. Many poor women were also placing bets in the hope of winning respite from poverty, and others were moving out of poverty by profiting from organising commercial gambling. Evidence regarding the extensive involvement of poorer women in organising illegal commercial gambling comes from the parliamentary inquiries into the State lottery, lottery insurances; the first in 1802 and the second in 1808. The Select Committees of 1802 and 1808 heard how the limited sale periods for tickets in the State Lottery was insufficient to satisfy the appetite of the public for this popular game of chance, encouraging illegal, penny lotteries, the "little goes" and "numbers clubs" that were found by the Select Committees to be hugely popular amongst the slum dwellers of London (P.P. 1808/9 Sessional Papers, Select Committee on Laws Relating to Lotteries, Second Report mf 9.11–12, p. 31). These were run, virtually unchecked, throughout the eighteenth and early-nineteenth centuries. Tickets were as little as a halfpenny, so the poorest in society could afford to play. The *Newgate Calendar* (11 August 1795) reported that:

> On Friday night last, in consequence of searching warrants ... upwards of thirty persons were apprehended at the house of one M'Call ... and in the house of J. Knight ... where the most destructive practices *to the poor* were carrying on, that of *Private Lotteries* (called Little Goes). ... The wives of many industrious mechanics, by attending these nefarious houses, have not only been duped out of their earnings (which ought to have been applied to the earning of bread for their families), but have even pawned their beds, wedding rings and almost every article they were possessed of, for that purpose.

The illegal insuring of State Lottery tickets was another form of numbers game of pure chance, and generally cost about one shilling per go in 1800, with the winner getting back £1 if the number insured was drawn. Conversely, the bet could be made that the number would not be drawn. The 1808 committee inquiring into lotteries concluded that each servant in London probably spent 25 shillings a year on illegal lotteries and insurances. The committee calculated that if all other wage-earning classes in the metropolis were spending similar amounts on such gambling then perhaps half a million pounds sterling was placed on various numbers games in London each year. Thus it can be understood that while the individual amounts staked were relatively small, the actual volume of such gambling was significant and widespread and was providing a very significant living for the entrepreneurs organising these gambling opportunities (P.P. 1808/9, Sessional Papers, Select Committee on Laws Relating to Lotteries, Second Report, mf 9.11–12, pp. 29–30).

Lotteries and their associated numbers games were immensely popular with women of the lower classes, and as the activity was illegal, women were regularly arrested and imprisoned for taking part in the games. One such illegal lottery saw the arrest of almost 400 participants, many of them women (P.P. 1808/9, Sessional Papers, Select Committee on Laws Relating to Lotteries, Second Report, mf 9.11–12, p. 53). It can be seen that even with a very small stake the participation of so many people in the lottery would provide both a good prize and an income for the organiser; and there were weekly draws. In evidence to the same committee, a magistrate, Mr Barker, spoke of the role of women employed in the illegal insurance of State Lottery tickets:

> A very considerable portion of women who could write and who know a little of figures, are employed in this nefarious trade; and whenever any of them are convicted and imprisoned, there is generally a stipulation with their principal that they shall be allowed two guineas per week during the term of their imprisonment. (P.P. 1808/9,

Sessional Papers, Select Committee on Laws Relating to Lotteries, Second Report, mf 9.11–12, p. 39)

The ability of these women, to stipulate that they be paid two guineas a week (when a labourer would earn around 12 shillings a week) during their imprisonment demonstrates the amount of income that could be made from this activity and also the degree of agency the women had in determining their value to the employer and the direction of their own lives.

Although the ending of the official lottery in 1826 also appears to have ended the lucrative business of insurances, Clapson (1991) points out that publicans were quick to fill the gap in the market with their own numbers games, and work by Clark (1983) Kirkby, (1997) and Wright, (2001) has illustrated how female publicans were in fact very prevalent. It is likely they found running gambling games or organising sporting activities on which people could gamble added to the profits of their business. However, the ending of the State Lottery was also the beginning of the proliferation of cash betting offices, especially in London and the major towns and cities (Clapson, 1991). Off-course betting provided an outlet for many of the poorer gamblers, and especially women gamblers, who would previously have engaged in gambling on illegal insurances, on lotteries, or in illegal lotteries (Miers, 1980, p. 171).

Steady pressure from the National Anti-Gambling League (NAGL), with many social reformers including B. S. Rowntree amongst its members, led to the establishment of a Royal Commission to investigate gambling. The 1902 House of Lords Commission on Gambling heard evidence regarding the extent of female involvement in gambling at all levels of society; "[a]t one end of the social scale costly jewellery is sold to cover bridge debts and at the other blankets pawned to put money on a horse" (Hogge, 1905, p. 69). As a result of the activities of the NAGL it was widely believed that gambling amongst the working classes was a significant cause of secondary poverty, and it was generally held that the running of gaming houses was almost entirely a female occupation; "[m]ore often than not it is managed by a woman" (Hogge, 1905, p. 82). The continued popularity of 'numbers games' organised by and for poor women was also an issue that concerned Parliament, the vicar of Jarrow on Tyne commented on gambling amongst women in his parish: "For the most part, it takes the form of lotteries or sweepstakes, women putting in their sixpences etc., and winning a possible twenty pounds or so" (Hogge, 1905, p. 74) and as with the illegal lotteries of the eighteenth century these sweeps were largely organised by women in the neighbourhood who made a profit from the game (Bell, 1907). There were reports to Parliament of women bookmakers in all major cities, and although women were a minority of bookmakers, they were nevertheless clearly using gambling as an opportunity to earn a living alongside, and it appears on an equal footing with, their male counterparts. There was little that could practically be done by the government to curb the gambling of the upper classes, for it largely took place in private, or even abroad, and was clearly beyond the jurisdiction of even the most fervent anti-gambling activist. However, the gambling habits of the working classes were in the process of being considered by Parliament. The prevailing opinion seems to have been that "their culture was degenerate and inferior. Their resort to gambling might have been understandable, but it was still grossly irrational" (Dixon, 1991, p. 42). Although the Royal Commission of 1902 found that gambling was a cross-class and cross-gender activity the resultant Street Betting Act (1906), which was the result of NAGL pressure and the parliamentary inquiry, was primarily designed to curtail the gambling activities of the working classes, a fact that was widely recognised at the time (Chinn, 1991; Clapson, 1991).

The Street Betting Act (1906) was not a success in curtailing gambling. During a raid on Bootle in 1915 the police observed 139 men, 85 women and 44 children entering an illegal betting office through the back door, while 18 men, 10 women, three boys and three girls entered by the front door (Clapson, 1991, p. 48). With illegal bookmaking such a significant feature of the black economy, and especially as it was closely linked with the retail trade via small, local shops, Clapson (1991) is certain that the numbers of women bookmakers are a hugely underestimated part of illegal street betting, and that this is an area that requires further investigation. Despite the illegality of the pastime, gambling remained a central feature of working-class activity for men and women in the interwar years with Orwell (1937) commenting that "[o]rganised gambling has now risen almost to the status of a major industry" (p. 80).

By the early-twentieth century a commercial leisure industry was also taking shape, providing legal leisure to the masses, and notable for the emergence of national chains in music halls, cinema, teashops and dance halls. In 1923 these operators were joined by the football pools, with John Moores's Littlewoods rapidly becoming a national institution. Moores was himself from a poor family and had first-hand knowledge of the importance of football gambling amongst poor men in particular. His experience of the place of gambling showed him that if he could develop a means of getting round the rules that prevented cash betting he could make a legal living from gambling. John Moores introduced the first widespread football pools venture from his family home in Manchester in 1922, but rapidly moved to Liverpool.

Printing coupons based upon the pre-announced fixtures list in advance allowed punters to pay by postal order, so the gamble was not strictly made in cash, and in addition, games of skill were not illegal. Moores argued that the pools required skill as this was not fixed-odds betting, but rather predictions of win, lose or draw (Clegg, 1993). The business started badly, but by the end of the 1926–1927 football season the pools begun to take off. The popularity of this gambling game was such that other commercial gambling companies then became established. The football pools expanded in the 1920s to such an extent that in 1928 the government legalised the activity, against the wishes of the Football Association who felt that allowing gambling on the results of matches would bring the game into disrepute. The football pools were immensely popular, so that by the 1930s an estimated £30 million annually was being gambled, mostly in 6*d.* postal orders, while the pools promoters employed about 30,000 people, the majority of whom were women (Walvin, 1994, pp. 126–128).

Although football gambling had moved into the commercial leisure industry by the interwar years, employing the working classes, rather than allowing them to develop opportunities for entrepreneurship, Elizabeth Roberts (1984) found that in Lancaster, Barrow and Preston during the same period many women acted as bookmakers or bookies' runners. One elderly blind woman in Lancaster earned a good living as a bookmaker. She used to leave her back door open, and bets were placed on the shelf by the door, a slip of paper wrapped round the stake (Centre for North West Regional Studies Elizabeth Roberts Archive, Mr N2L RSC 88/562). She was never prosecuted for running her illegal business because the local police officers placed their bets with her. There are similar examples of working-class women who were running illegal cash betting enterprises from around the UK, Rose

Working-Class Gambling Entrepreneurs

Pickering was "a popular bookie in Birmingham"(Birmingham Lives Carl Chinn Archive) and Mrs Eyres ran a book from her greengrocery shop in Moseley Street, ensuring a steady supply of customers in 1926. Credit bookmaking was not illegal and the 1921 census recorded 2,824 male bookmakers and 73 female. By 1931 numbers had trebled to 9,330 men and 425 women (Huggins, 2000). These figures do not include those operating illegal cash betting enterprises.

Big Business and Gambling

Although there was extensive small-scale commercialisation of gambling over the period 1660–1960, the legal status of gambling meant that while other leisure activities, such as the music hall, rapidly developed into national chains (Kift, 1996) organised to benefit from economies of scale in the nineteenth century, it was not until the development of a model of football pools that mitigated the prohibitions on fixed-odds betting (that was developed by John Moores) that there was the beginning of a national commercial gambling industry. After the Second World War the spread of holiday camps (Ward & Hardy, 1986), commercial dance halls (Nott, 2002) and the increasing development of cinema chains (Spraos, 1962) was accompanied by pressure to relax the anti-gambling legislation. This pressure included significant lobbying by Butlins who had found operating bingo as a recreation for campers at their holiday camps to be hugely lucrative. They had to donate the proceeds to charity, and in 1957 National Playing Fields received over £50,000. Almost as soon as gambling was legalised on 1 January 1961 Mecca moved into bingo and rapidly dominated the market (Downs, 2010) as it, and other operators, exploited a series of loopholes in the poorly drafted gaming part of the Betting and Gaming Act (1960). Meanwhile in bookmaking the independents survived on many high streets. In part this was a result of the legislation regarding betting shops having been carefully thought through and designed to meet the needs of a well-understood demand for cash betting that would in many instances be supplied by the street-bookmakers moving into regulated premises. The transfer into licensed premises required under the provisions of the Betting and Gaming Act (1960) immediately acted as a barrier to women (who in general were providing bookmaking from their homes or shops, and who were not in a position to fulfil either the requirements for a licence or for a formal operating environment with fixed hours of work). Specifically, it did not provide the flexibility to allow women to combine bookmaking with their other responsibilities. The development of large chains of bookmakers that dominate the High Street today was much slower than the development of a commercial gaming industry dominated by national chains which emerged within a year of the legalisation of commercial gaming, and was complete by 1968 (Downs, 2010).

Conclusions
Governments regulate many activities that can be categorised as vices in order to ensure social control. The level of regulation is dependent on a range of variables that might include religious or moral precepts, degree of harm caused by the vice or public pressure for control. In the case of gambling there was a class-based approach to regulation from the early-nineteenth century, with the aim of preventing the poor from gambling while allowing the wealthy to make their own decisions. However, the desire of the masses to gamble meant that the imperatives of capitalism operated to ensure a market developed and many working-class men and a significant number of women were able to exploit the commercial

potential of gambling and used it as a means of earning an income. Gambling entrepreneurship amongst women throughout many periods in history can be used as a tool to illustrate the degree of control that women were able to have over their own lives. Gambling women could also be considered to prove the anthropological assertion that gambling is linked to a "high frequency of responsible behaviour and high frequency of achievement behaviour" (Roberts, Arth, & Bush, 1959, p. 604). For problem gamblers aside, all the evidence points to the working classes, both men and women, using gambling both as an exciting form of leisure and a profitable business opportunity since at least the late seventeenth century.

References

Ashton, J. (1898). *The history of gambling in England*. London, United Kingdom: Duckworth.

Bailey, P. (1987). *Leisure and class in Victorian England: Rational recreation and the contest for control*. London, United Kingdom: Routledge.

Beckwith, L. (1971). *About my father's business*. London, United Kingdom: Arrow Books.

Bell, F. E. E. O. (1907). *At the works: A study of a manufacturing town*. London, United Kingdom: Edward Arnold.

Birley, S. (1988). School Working Paper 5187: Female entrepreneurs – are they really any different? Retrieved from: https://dspace.lib.cranfield.ac.uk/retrieve/1085/SWP3187.pdf

Bradley, H. (1989). *Men's work, women's work: A sociological history of the sexual division of labour in employment*. Minneapolis, MN: University of Minnesota Press.

Cantillon, R. (1755). *Essai sur la nature du commerce engénéral (Essay on the Nature of Trade in General)*. Retrieved from http://www.econlib.org/library/NPDBooks/Cantillon/cntNTCover.html

Casey, E. (2003). Gambling and consumption: Working-class women and UK National Lottery play. *Journal of Consumer Culture*, 3(2), 245–263.

Chinn, C. (1991). *Better betting with a decent feller: Betting, bookmaking and the British working class, 1750–1990*. Hemel Hempstead, United Kingdom: Harvester.

Clapson, M. (1991). *A bit of a flutter: Popular gambling in England, 1823–1961*. Manchester, United Kingdom: Manchester University Press.

Clark, P. (1983). *The English alehouse – a social history 1200–1830*. London, United Kingdom: Longman.

Clegg, B. (1993). *The man who made Littlewoods: The story of John Moores*. London, United Kingdom: Hodder & Stoughton.

Coleman, M. (2005). A terrible danger to the morals of the country: The Irish hospitals sweepstake in Great Britain, 1930–87. *Proceedings of the Royal Irish Academy, Section C, 105*(1), 197–220.

Cross, G. S. (1993). *Time and money: The making of consumer culture*. London, United Kingdom: Taylor & Francis.

Dawson, E. (1962). *Mother made a book*. London, United Kingdom: Geoffrey Bles.

DeMartino, R., & Barbato, R. (2003). Differences between women and men MBA entrepreneurs: Exploring family flexibility and wealth creation as career motivators. *Journal of Business Venturing, 18*(6), 815–832.

Dixon, D. (1991). *From prohibition to regulation: Anti-gambling and the law*. Oxford, United Kingdom: Clarendon.

Downs, C. (2009). *A social, economic and cultural history of bingo (1906-2005): The role of gambling in the lives of working women*. Saarbrücken, Germany: VDM Verlag.

Downs, C. (2010). Mecca and the birth of commercial bingo 1958–70: A case study. *Business History, 52*(7), 1086–1106.

Hisrich, R. D., & Brush, C. G. (1985). Women and minority entrepreneurs: A comparative analysis. In J. Hornaday, E. Shills, J. Timmons & K. Vesper (Eds.), *Frontiers of Entrepreneurship Research*, (pp. 566–587). Babson Park, MA: Babson College.

Hogge, J. M. (1905). Gambling among women. In B. S. Rowntree (Ed.), *Betting and gambling: A national evil* (pp. 69–83). London, United Kingdom: Macmillan.

Huggins, M. (2000) *Flat racing and British society 1790–1914: A social and economic history*. London, United Kingdom: Frank Cass.

Kempson, E. (1996). *Life on a low income*. York, United Kingdom: York Publishing Services for Joseph Rowntree Foundation.

Kemsley, W. F. F., & Ginsburg, D. (1951). *Betting in Britain 1949–1950*. London, United Kingdom: Central Office of Information.

Kift, D. (1996). *The Victorian music hall: Culture, class and conflict* (2nd ed.). Cambridge, United Kingdom: Cambridge University Press.

Kirkby, D. (1997). *Barmaids: A history of women's work in pubs*. Cambridge, United Kingdom: Cambridge University Press.

Kopf, E. W. (1927). The early history of the annuity. *Proceedings of the Casualty Actuarial Society, 13*, 225–266.

Kowalski, W. J. (2000). Roman Board Games. Retrieved from http://ablemedia.com/ctcweb/showcase/boardgames8.html

Liles, P. R. (1974). *New business ventures and the entrepreneur*. East Lansing, MI: Michigan State University.

Miers, D. (1980). Eighteenth century gaming: Implications for modern casino control. In J. A. Inciardi, & C. E. Faupel (Eds.), *History and crime* (pp. 169–192). London, United Kingdom: Heinemann.

Milani-Santarpia, G. (2011). Roman Entertainment and Games. Retrieved from http://www.mariamilani.com/ancient_rome/ancient_roman_games_entertainment.htm

Mill, J. S. (1848). *Principles of political economy with some of their applications to social philosophy*. Manchester, United Kingdom: George Routledge and Sons.

Milsom, S. F. C. (1981). *The nature of Blackstone's achievements*. London, United Kingdom: Seldon Society.

Myers, D. G. (2000). Hope and happiness. In M. E. Seligman & J. Gillham. (Eds.), *The science of optimism and hope: Research essays in honor of Martin E. P. Seligman: Volume 2* (pp. 323–337). West Conshohocken, PA: Philadelphia Templeton Foundation Press.

Nott, J. (2002). *Music for the people*. Oxford, United Kingdom: Oxford University Press.

Orwell, G. (1937). *The road to Wigan Pier*. London, United Kingdom: Victor Gollancz.

Radford, P. (2001). *The celebrated Captain Barclay: Sport, money and fame in Regency Britain*. London, United Kingdom: Headline.

Roberts, E. (1984). *A woman's place: An oral history of working-class women 1890–1940*. Oxford, United Kingdom: Blackwell Publishing.

Roberts, E. (1995). *Women and families: An oral history, 1940–1970*. Cambridge, MA: Blackwell Publishing.

Roberts, J. M., Arth, M. J., & Bush, R. R. (1959). Games in culture. *American Anthropologist, 61*(4), 597–605.

Rowntree, B. S. (1901). *Poverty: A study of town life 1830–1890*. London, United Kingdom: Policy Press.

Rowntree, B. S. (1941). *Poverty and progress: A second social survey of York*. London, United Kingdom: Longmans, Green & Co.

Russell, G. (2000). Faro's daughters: Female gamesters, politics and the discourse of finance in 1790s Britain. *Eighteenth Century Studies, 33*(4), 481–505.

Schumpeter, J. A. (1954). *History of economic analysis*. New York, NY: Oxford University Press.

Smart, C., & Neale, B (1999). *Family fragments*. Cambridge, United Kingdom: Polity.

Smart, C. (2007). *Personal life*. Cambridge, United Kingdom: Polity Press.

Sonnenberg, S. J. (2008). Household financial organisation and discursive practice: Managing money and identity. *Journal of Socio-Economics, 37*(2), 533–551.

Spraos, J. (1962). *The decline of the cinema*. London, United Kingdom: Allen & Unwin.

Thompson, E. P. (1961). *The making of the English working class*. Harmondsworth, United Kingdom: Penguin.

Walvin, J. (1994). *The People's Game*, London, United Kingdom: Allen Lane.

Ward, C., & Hardy, D. (1986). *Goodnight campers! The history of the British holiday camp*. London, United Kingdom: Mansell Publishing Limited.

Wardle, H. (2007). *British gambling prevalence survey 2007*. Birmingham, United Kingdom: National Centre for Social Research.

Wright, C. (2001). Of public houses and private lives: Female hotelkeepers as domestic entrepreneurs. *Australian Historical Studies, 32*(116), 57–75.

Zweig, F. (1948). *Life, labour and poverty*. London, United Kingdom: Gollancz.
Zweig, F. (1952). *Women's life and labour*. London, United Kingdom: Gollancz.
Zweig, F. (1961). *The worker in an affluent society*. London, United Kingdom: Heinemann.

CHAPTER 5

'THE BUZZ WAS EVERY BIT AS GOOD AS THE PRIZE, IF NOT MORE': A FORMER CAREER CRIMINAL'S PERSPECTIVE ON RISK

Karen Corteen and Eric Allison

This chapter discusses two areas, namely 'career criminality' and 'risk'. Both feature highly in the discipline of criminology and indeed they also figure prominently in debates, policies and state practices with regard to crime, crime prevention and harm avoidance. More recently the career criminal has been discussed in relation to penal thinking, penal practices and risk. Yet, the actual experiences of risk on the part of career criminals is somewhat neglected in criminological literature.[1] This chapter contains the perspective and experiences of Eric Allison, a former 'career criminal' who had been imprisoned a number of times for crimes such as robbery and fraud. It depicts his experience of, and perspectives on, risk and the role that risk played in his criminal career. The chapter will briefly discuss the manner in which risk has come to occupy a significant place in criminological theorising and penal thinking and practices. A succinct discussion of the career criminal approach will follow. After introducing Eric Allison and providing some relevant background information, Allison's views on the role of risk in his former criminal career will be discussed. The discussion will be organised around the

---

[1] Katz (1988) is somewhat of an exception here. Although Katz's (1988) research on the experiences of offenders in the commission of crime, including career criminals, did reveal that risk-taking was thrilling, the intention of his research was not to specifically explore the role of risk amongst career criminals.

themes of risk assessment and avoidance and risk seeking and embracement.

Criminology Meets the Risk Society
The concept of risk can be traced back to Beck's (1992) groundbreaking book on the 'risk society'. For Beck, society in late-modernity is a risk society and this is a perpetual state of affairs. In a nutshell, Beck's stance is that because of a fear of risks people demand more and more information about risks and this in turn identifies more behaviours, substances, people and events that individuals and identifiable groups are at risk from. In the attempt to control future risk, risk (and agendas surrounding its management) is further heightened (Giddens, 1999). So rather than the introduction of technological developments to provide insurances against risks – making society feel more certain and secure about the world – "the opposite is true" (Giddens, 1999, p. 1).

O'Malley (2010) explains that the revelation of new risks has resulted in a "further heightening of risk consciousness and a vicious circle of fear and securitization" (p. 12). Subsequently risk-induced fears evoke calls for greater securitisation in all areas of social life. For Risley (2006) "among the many realms becoming progressively securitised are migration, protest, policing, penalty, urban restructuring, the environment, public health, and even disaster response" (p. 1).

Within criminological thinking the concept of risk has been theorised dualistically. On the one hand, criminological responses to risk are in recognition of the criminal justice system's and other institutions' obsession with risk identification, risk management, risk reduction and subsequently crime prevention, crime reduction, crime minimisation and the prevention of harm (Farrall, Bottoms, &

'The Buzz Was Every Bit as Good as the Prize'

Shapland, 2010; Feeley & Simon, 1992; Garland, 1996, 2001; O'Malley, 2010). This has been attributed to the emergence of new penology (Feeley & Simon, 1992). New penology encapsulates changes in penal thinking and penal practices from a concern with individual causes of crime and the rehabilitative ideal, to a concern with the risk of crime and actuarial minimisation of such risks through systematic predication of identifiable 'risky' groups (O'Malley, 2010; Slingeneyer, 2007). O'Malley (2010) states, "[b]y the end of the twentieth century, risk had become a predominant way of governing all manner of problems. Prevention is better than cure" (p. 3). This can be evidenced throughout the criminal justice system.

Risk, however, has to be understood in different contexts, thus whilst in the public, political and state actors' imaginations it is something to be predicted, avoided and managed, it can also be imagined or reconfigured as something more positive. This can be seen in a second or alternative response to risk; this comprises the recognition of the practical engagement in and theorisation of risk as legitimate and illegitimate risk-taking for thrills, excitement and pleasure (Ferrell, 2005; Ferrell, Milovanovic, & Lyng, 2001; Lyng, 1990, 2004, 2005).

Such voluntary risk-taking has been interpreted in different ways. O'Malley (2010) explains how positivist criminologists have pathologised such activity in that they have explained this as either down to a person's own innate failings or a pathological response to a worker's routinised lives and the mundane lives of the poor. In contrast to this, Katz (1988) recognises the seduction of crime and in so doing he argues that risk and risk-taking can be read as creative, exciting, thrilling and as resistance. Engagement in risk also cuts across the social classes and therefore cannot be reduced simply to a class phenomenon.

Retaining the embodied and visceral elements of Katz (1988), cultural criminologists contextualise crime and crime control in relation to culture. Cultural criminologists explore meaning, emotions, style, symbols, signifying practices and identity as well as media culture (Ferrell, 1995). They also examine legal and illegal embracing of risk, conceiving risk-taking as 'edgework' and as a form of resistance to authority (Ferrell, 2005; Hebdige, 1979; Lyng, 2004, 2005). This is evidenced in examples such as: an engagement in legitimate or illegitimate 'extreme sports' such as skydiving, BASE jumping[2] (Ferrell et al., 2001) or engaging in risky occupations (Lyng, 2004). The focus is the embodied, emotional, voluntary, and transgressive aspects of sub-cultural risk-taking and risk-embracing. Indeed for cultural criminologists efforts to prevent or stop 'edgeworkers' serve to heighten the risk and subsequently enhance the thrill of their 'edgy' activities (Ferrell, 2005; Ferrell, Haywood, & Young, 2008). Embracing and engaging in risk produces countercultures and challenges the dominant culture (Hebdige, 1979; Ferrell & Saunders, 1995; Ferrell, Hayward, Morrison, & Presdee, 2004; Ferrell et al., 2008). A by-product or an unintended outcome of a postmodern society's desire for security and its emphasis on risk-containment is resistance to the culture of control through the embracing and taking of risk (Hebdige, 1979; Ferrell & Saunders, 1995; Ferrell, et al., 2004; Lyng, 2004, 2005; Ferrell, 2005; Ferrell et al., 2008; O'Malley, 2010).

To summarise, on the one hand criminologists and state actors have approached risk in terms of the fear it induces and

---

[2] The illegal parachuting off various obstacles, for example bridges and cliffs (Lyng, 2005).

the response it provokes in the form of risk management rooted in a culture of crime and crime control and in a culture of "punitive interventionism" (Bell, 2010, para. 3). This has led to a restructuring of the criminal justice system and emphasis on "offender management" and "financial efficiency" rather than individual rehabilitation (Bell, 2010 para. 7). An actuarial new penology has emerged wherein the role of the criminal justice system and other agents of control are less concerned with the correction of the individual offender and more geared towards "risk-reducing incapacitation or warehousing" (O'Malley, 2010, p. 5). The incapacitative continuum comprises the identification and management of aggregate groups of risky populations.

On the other hand the cultural criminologist and those who engage in risk-taking, perceive risk as 'edgework', comprising of a transgressive, emotional, embodied, visceral subcultural experience, which is thrilling, pleasurable, exciting and even a spectacle and carnivalesque. It can also be interpreted as resistance and illustrative of a counterculture.

The Criminal Career Approach
Within criminology there is a perspective called the criminal career approach; it focuses on 'criminal careers' and 'career criminals' (Blumstein, Cohen, Roth, & Vischer, 1986). 'Career criminal' is a term that is frequently used in the media and is used by the public in a way that fails to acknowledge the societal, criminological and legal significance of the career criminal[3] (see DeLisi, 2005). Soothill, Fitzpatrick, and Frances (2009) define a career criminal approach as the study of "a few high-rate or long-duration offenders who do make a career out of crime" (p. 3). The last decade or so has witnessed a renewed

---

[3] There are dissenting voices amongst criminologists who explore career criminals (see DeLisi, 2005, for a more in-depth discussion).

interest in this area as a result of technological advances in statistical analysis. Also of late, with regard to the criminal career, it can be seen that risk, as conceptualised in new penology, has influenced the manner in which the career criminal is conceptualised in penal thinking and practice. However, the degree to which this is the case in relation to the conceptualisation of risk as 'edgework' and something to be embraced is far less.

DeLisi (2005) and Soothill et al. (2009) recognise that the criminal career approach is a controversial area, notwithstanding it is an important focus of criminology in the USA and in the UK. The career criminal approach emerged out of the US National Academy of Science Panel on Criminal Career Research (Blumstein et al., 1986). Primarily it is a quantitative approach that is not an exact science due to its reliance on data from official crime statistics and self-report studies – both of which are problematic (Farrington, 1992, 2003). There are however, some qualitative studies in this area and some theorists have begun using a mixed method approach (see Soothill et al., 2009). Therefore a traditional criminal career approach investigates the careers of criminals including career criminals.

A career criminal is defined by Farrington (1992) as "the longitudinal sequence of offences committed by an individual offender" (p. 521). A traditional career criminal approach strives to document offending over an individual's life course. In so doing it tends to be somewhat of a 'number crunching' enterprise in which criminologists statistically plot the start, end, duration and continuation of criminal careers (see Farrington, 2003 for example). Thus they are predominantly concerned with "onset, persistence and desistence" (Soothill et al., 2009, p. xiii). Soothill et al. (2009) point out that the concepts of onset, persistence and desistence are not straightforward. For example what constitutes the 'onset' of crime – the first time a child recognises that they committed a crime, the first time someone notices the child has committed an offence or the first time they are officially convicted of committing a crime?

In the main such studies in criminals' careers and career criminals have concentrated on (male) teenagers or juvenile delinquents as this is deemed to be the peak age in which offending occurs and most teenagers desist from committing crime as they enter into adulthood. From research on career criminals it can be deduced that such a career may actually entail the commission of one offence or the commission of many over time. Also career criminals are many and varied (see the works of Farrington, 1992, 2003: an authority on this subject).[4] The issue of desistance is also complex and studies have become more sophisticated (see for example the work of Farrall, Bottoms, & Shapland, 2010 and Farrall, Sharpe, Hunter, & Calverley, 2011).[5] Longitudinal career criminal studies have documented the prevalence of crime and the predictors, causes and correlations of crime (Farrington, 2003). Since the 1990s criminologists have concentrated on risk-focused prevention – a product of the new penological turn discussed above.

Career criminals, while not dissimilar to those that were previously conceptualised as 'habitual offenders' or the

---

[4] Also see Soothill et al.'s, 2009 book, which, attempts to bring together the study of career criminals, criminological theory and policy-related studies.

[5] Farrall and Calverley (2006) note that although work on desistance drew on the insights generated from research into criminal careers by the mid-1980s, the investigation of desistance became a legitimate area of its own as opposed to an 'appendage to research on criminal careers' (p. 4).

'professional criminals' are however, somewhat different (Slingeneyer, 2007). This too is largely a result of new penology and the emphasis that has been placed on risk (Feeley & Simon, 1992).[6] Thus it is not the identification or treatment of the underlying or external causes of career criminality that underpin penal thinking or practices "but rather the identification of the rate of risk of the offender and of determining the penal measure that corresponds to it" (Slingeneyer, 2007, para. 27).

Farrall et al. (2010) would concur with this contention; they assert that "the central message of the risk-based approach is not 'do good' but 'prevent harm' (p. 560). Thus attempts on the part of the state actors to assess risk and prevent the resultant harms from such risks, as opposed to rehabilitating the individual, may impact on an individual's capacity to desist from crime (Farrall et al., 2010). For example, this may be seen in disproportionate precautionary measures and increasing punitiveness including incarceration; systems that are risk-driven and may over-ride or undermine rehabilitative offender-focused responses.

There has been (and still is) substantial criminological interest in the risks that subcultural groups enjoy and embrace, and there remains a focus on how the agents of social control attempt to identify, manage and limit risk with regard to crime; this includes career criminality. Less interest has been paid to the relationship that career criminals have with risk. This chapter now proceeds to discuss how one former career criminal, Eric Allison, experienced risk in his high-risk

---

[6] There is not so much as a shift from 'old' to 'new' penology, but an intensification of punishment (Sim, 2009) and other criminal justice practices in keeping with new, as opposed to old, penology.

career and it does so through the themes of risk assessment and risk avoidance and risk seeking and embracement. Firstly however, Eric is introduced and some necessary background information is provided.

Eric Allison – A Tale of Two Interconnected Trajectories: From Professional Career Criminal and Prisoner to Professional Investigative Journalist and Prison Campaigner

The first author of this chapter, Karen Corteen, first came across the work of Eric Allison when she read his excellent co-authored book on the Strangeways disturbances (Jameson & Allison, 1995). This, together with his investigative journalism, in his role as Prison Correspondent for *The Guardian* and *The Guardian Unlimited* (http://www.guardian.co.uk/profile/ericallison), made him an ideal respondent for a research project that Corteen and Barton were undertaking entitled, *Researching Crime and State Power: Political, Practical and Ethical Realities*.[7] As part of this project Allison was interviewed on 25 January 2008; some of the material from that interview will be conveyed below. This chapter highlights what a 'risky business' being a career criminal can be – being both a serious consideration and an exciting endeavour; but first a little more about Allison.[8]

---

[7] The project was designed and conducted by Dr Alana Barton (Edge Hill University) and Dr Karen Corteen. It entailed tailored, semi-structured interviews with academics, lawyers, investigative journalists, documentary makers and campaigners engaged in critical social research as part of their professional engagement in activities geared towards social change.

[8] The narrative that Allison provides in this chapter is drawn from transcriptions of interviews and from a conference workshop presented at the University of Chester.

Although Allison's role as Prison Correspondent was initially salaried, Allison now works on a freelance contract and this gives him the independence and freedom to select his 'own stories' and areas for commentary pieces. Although due to media imperatives (such as newsworthiness, threshold and proximity for example) (Jewkes, 2011), not everything that he writes finds its way into *The Guardian* or elsewhere. In a research interview, Allison notes, "[t]here isn't much sunshine in this job – it's very difficult to get positive things in [newspapers] about prisons". In his role as prison correspondent Allison has exposed various injustices within, and problems related to, the secure estate, including unprofessional conduct (see for example Allison, 2012a, 2012b, 2012c, 2013). His role is very much an interventionist one; intervening to bring about positive change is his primary motivation for doing the job and he has no intention of giving up the fight for change. He has also written two fictional books, which constitute part of the crime genre. Further, Allison writes pieces for various local newspapers and campaign journals such as *Fight Racism, Fight Imperialism*, has been involved in documentaries and is regularly invited to speak at conferences.

The year 2003 proved to be one of a hiatus for Allison; *The Guardian* advertised for a prison correspondent and it welcomed applications from ex-offenders – Allison heard about the vacancy in a serendipitous manner.[9] After a series of interviews Allison was offered the job. However, he did not

---

[9] According to Allison, getting the position at *The Guardian* 'was a complete accident'. Whilst Eric has always been an avid reader of the paper, he never looked at the jobs section because he 'had a job'. It was a friend of his who alerted him to the job advert.

accept this position immediately; he had to "really think about it" as "it meant a complete change of everything – it meant going from being steeped in crime to having nothing to do with it other than writing and researching about it". Although being a prison correspondent for *The Guardian* was "not really" on Allison's "horizon", and he felt that in some respects he was ill-equipped for the job, his former belief in, and commitment to, the adage that "the pen is mightier than the sword" meant that Eric had useful insights with regard to his new career. His direct experience of prison as a prisoner together with his campaign writing whilst inside and outside of prison meant that Eric was well placed to take up this new role. Eric only realised how much he actually knew about the prison and prison activism when he began the job. Allison's tenacity, integrity and sense of justice regarding his investigations and campaign work have earned him a prestigious reputation as a staunch, yet informed critic of the criminal justice system, especially the secure estate. The difference in this role is that significantly he now has the 'power of the press' which helps to open doors to which he would not have previously had access (and he now he gets paid for exposing harms and injustices).

Over time in a professional capacity Allison has developed "good sources", in places [such as hospitals and], in prisons including whistleblowers, whom he would "never reveal" or "compromise". He acknowledges that he has a duty of care to those less powerful individuals who come into contact with the criminal justice system as either offenders or victims or both. Usually both, as in Allison's experience, "nine times out of ten the line between victims and offenders is very thin. The offenders are often victims". His moral code in his current employment is an extension of his moral code as a career criminal. He enjoys the "good name" that he has earned as an investigative journalist in a similar manner to having a "good name as a criminal and prison activist". Also whilst Allison "used to work hard at crime" since he began this occupation he has "never worked so hard in [his] life". He is committed to the cause of exposing unprofessional and harmful practices within state institutions, particularly the secure estate via *The Guardian* newspaper; a paper which he respects and from which he himself gains respect as a result of his association with it.

The offer of the job together with his familial relationships in 2003 meant that Allison gave up a career as a professional criminal – however, he has not turned his back on crime. Indeed he acknowledges that in his endeavours as an investigative journalist researching the criminal justice system and systemic injustices he still over-identifies with prisoners and offenders, stating that he is "very offender-based". Indeed Allison commented that, "funny enough I often feel more like a prisoner now than I ever did when I was in prison because it surrounds me all the time and I am immersed in it". He continued stating, "I empathise completely with prisoners … too much really. It's an obsession more than a job." He explained why he felt more like a prisoner now than he did in prison: "because in prison I wasn't in prison mentally you see, in a way, but now I am. It's funny, a bit strange." That said, central to his personal and professional politics are victims and society and understanding why individuals commit crime in order to "prevent further crime and victimization". Although Allison's current employment does not "pay as well as crime" and his "standard of living has gone down" he would not "swap" his current occupation, "sometimes not even for the keys of the Bank of England".

In relation to his former life as a criminal, he comments "I'd been a criminal all my life. I am not proud of it and I'm

'The Buzz Was Every Bit as Good as the Prize'

not ashamed of it, it's what I was." At the time when the position of Prison Correspondent at *The Guardian* arose Eric was "taking a bit of a sabbatical", he thought that he would "take it easy for a while" and "make better contact" with his daughters. He was also of the opinion that he "was going to be a criminal for the rest [of his] life". When the position "came along" Eric was actually "considering offers" (to get involved in criminal operations) and if he had not secured the position at *The Guardian* he has no doubt that he would "still be involved in a life of crime". He stated, "I would definitely have carried on because that's all I could do, and it's what I knew. ... I would have carried on, I just never dreamt of this [being a Prison Correspondent]." Eric likes "living on the edge" and he used to get "a buzz from crime" but he now gets "a bigger buzz" from working as a Prison Correspondent. His desistance from committing crime is not that he has "turned from a life of crime" but that he has "just found something that gives [him] a better buzz" and without it he "would have still been bang at it. Absolutely." The final part of this chapter will now focus on Allison's criminal career and the role of risk.

Career Criminality –'A Risky Business'

The following section presents the thoughts and perspectives of Allison captured during an audio recorded workshop presentation with Corteen in March 2012. Here Allison reflects that it has been 12 years (at the time of writing) since he has been in prison and during that time he has been a productive law-abiding citizen. It was not Allison's intention to enter into a career of crime, this was not what he "set out to do". His entry into crime is relayed:

> When I was young, I just went wrong, if you like. I made bad choices and was nicked a couple of times. I'm a great believer that if you constantly tell young people that they're

bad, even when they aren't, they embrace that badness. And that's what I did. At quite an early age, once I'd been away, and I had a couple of custodial sentences, I realised that they [prisons for children] didn't have any crocodiles or anything in there. I thought "I can cope with it". Also there's an old saying, 'If you can't do the time, don't do the crime.' And that was my motto. So I embarked on a career in crime and I wanted to be a good criminal.

Allison's "own set of moral boundaries" in the commission of crime and in relation to other criminals is very important (Allison, 2008, 25 January; Allison, 2012, 6 March). There are "some crimes" that Eric "would never commit", he would never "use gratuitous violence" he would "never set out to be violent to anybody"; however, he has "used the threat of violence" and he has used it "to escape on a couple of occasions, to avoid being apprehended" (Allison, 2012, 6 March). He admits that he used to tell himself that due to the types of crime he committed that there "were no victims" but he knows now "that, that's a load of rubbish, of course", but they were not victims of violence. In the main Eric has worked by himself, but he has worked with other career criminals.

In 1996 (one year after the publication of his book on the Strangeways disturbances) he was sent back to Strangeways for a number of offences including stealing £1 million from a high street bank in Manchester. Allison has been in and out of prison since he was a young child. His first crime was "stealing pennies out of a bubble gum machine" (Allison, 2008, 25 January) – he was caught and sent to a Detention Centre and whilst incarcerated (then and thereafter) he learned about crime and over the years his crimes progressed and he ended his criminal career as a professional fraudster. He "moved towards fraud as he got older" because he was getting older and also "the potential prize was still very, very good but the penalties for white collar crime were a lot smaller" (Allison, 2012, 6 March). The risk of long prison sentences became more significant with age as there is less time left to complete the prison sentence. He comments that when he was single and in his thirties he would take the risk of doing 10 to 12 years in prison but he would not take that risk in his fifties.

With regard to risk, Allison contends that crime is a "risky business" for career criminals and that career criminals have "always known there is a risk and they do take risk into account". When he was assessing the level of risk in relation to a job he would "take into account" the prize, the risk of being caught, the nature of the job (in terms of dangerousness) and how long he would be sent to prison for if he was caught. He contends that although "most criminals" he knows "do take risk very much into account" this does not always prevent them from getting caught. Weighing up the risk or taking risk into account may go some way towards career criminals having to "face the reality" of the "consequences of getting caught". However, such a rational assessment of risk appears to be undercut by the ever-present "hope or belief that you won't get caught". Allison believes that the percentage of career criminals who plan their operations meticulously is very low and although they do pay attention to detail with regard to averting the risk of getting caught and managing the risk on the job he questions whether career criminals including himself are "balanced". He questions the degree of rationality involved in the decision to commit crime due to degree of risk involved and because of what is actually at stake, namely one's liberty. He equates putting his "freedom" at risk with gambling noting that it is the same kind of "buzz and thrill" as when you gamble. It is the "anticipation" and the "waiting to see if you have pulled it off, whether it is a job or a bet on the horses or the dogs".

Also Allison maintains that no one is above risk-taking. After a discussion with students in a workshop about cultural representations of Mr Big (a distanced individual orchestrating others to perpetrate crime from which the individual profits) Allison comments:

> In my experience Mr Big does not exist outside the pages of fiction. Because no self-respecting criminal would take orders from somebody and allow that person to take a bigger share of the profits without taking risk. ... When putting together an operation, with what we use to call "a small firm of thieves", everyone takes a risk so everyone gets some of the profit. There was nobody in the firm who got more than anyone else even though on lots of occasions, because of their expertise and ability some people would do more work than others.

He reiterates "my motto has always been if a person takes the risk then they get an equal share of the prize" and that despite an unequal distribution of work due to ability and expertise "in the end, all the firms that I worked with, everybody got their equal share. And that was very important." He continues: "[b]ecause prison was very much part and parcel of crime, an occupational hazard if you like, the idea of a Mr Big who pulls the strings and never takes that risk [imprisonment], just doesn't exist in my experience".

In order to reinforce that no one does "not put themselves on offer" in the risky business of career criminality he cites various infamous career criminals who got caught and went to prison, for example the Krays and Ronnie Biggs. He believes that criminals who are "the head of an organisation" as opposed to a Mr Big-like caricature, actually take greater risks due to the "massive amount of attention" they receive from

'The Buzz Was Every Bit as Good as the Prize'

the public and from the authorities. This amount of attention means that when high profile, or celebrity criminals, do get caught they are subjected to "very long sentences"; when they "do get nicked, they [the authorities] tend to throw away the key". Thus, whilst there may be higher-up criminals who control the criminal organisation or the operation of a job, "they, like most people get their hands dirty in that they take risks and put their liberty on the line".

Allison asserts that when there is "more than one [person]" on a job then there is a heightened risk as "basically you are putting your liberty in the hands of somebody else ... there are a lot of informers ... in a way, it's almost like a normal job, you come across good people and you come across bad people". In order to avert the risk of working with "bad people" Allison would "test" any "new people" he worked with. He expands, "I would give them the opportunity to rip me off, a very small amount. And if and when they did, I used to actually thank them, because they had showed me inside their soul. It may have cost me money, but years down the line it could have cost me a lot of time in prison."

Career criminals also seek out and embrace risk in a visceral sense according to Allison. When asked if career criminals engaged in risk-taking for pleasure during his criminal career he replied:

> Yes they do. I used to get a buzz from crime, as I said when I was a kid, I just went wrong. I never really thought about crime, you know, it's only later on in life when I've made this conscious decision to live outside the law. And yeah, I used to get a thrill from it, there's no question about it. And to be perfectly honest with you, I sometimes miss it, because it was a special buzz.

He becomes quite animated and he continues with this line of thought, stating:

> It wasn't just getting the money. I mean, money wasn't really important to me, it's never been important to me. Getting the prize was good of course it's always nice to be successful in getting the prize that you were aiming for. But it was the carrying it out, knowing full well that you're doing something, that you're going to be putting yourself in danger. And danger is quite a nice place to be sometimes, if you can manage it. So yes, I think criminals certainly do embrace risk and I think it is very much part and parcel of it. … Without a doubt I think the thrill of risk is a big factor.

Allison revisits and retells the buzz that he gets from his role as a prison correspondent. He enjoys "digging out", "pursuing" and "exposing" wrongdoing and injustice in the criminal justice system especially with regard to deaths in custody and miscarriages of justice. He also emphasised that he "is not trying to say 'oh, I was badly done to as a kid' and that is why I went into crime originally". He continued, "I'm quite happy with my life. I've had a very rich and interesting life. I mean even the bad times have been very interesting. So I'm not complaining about it". He remains however, "very angry" that as a society we continue to lock people up, especially children and that society does not appear to "have learnt anything" from the "damage done" from incarcerating individuals, and women and children in particular. For example, speaking about private secure detention centres especially, he stated, "it drives me forward in the same way that I used to be driven to crime – I used to think 'let's get the prize', now I want to nail these buggers, those who are making vast profits out of locking up damaged young children".

Towards the end of the workshop Allison talked some more about the buzz, in trepidation and excitement of waiting

'The Buzz Was Every Bit as Good as the Prize'

to see if a criminal operation had been successful; he talked about the subsequent come-down from that. He confirmed the amount of "ground work" and "months of planning" that had been put into the theft from the high street bank of £1 million pounds and the enjoyment in the final "suspense" of waiting to see if "the cheques had cleared" and if he was to be "paid out". He goes on to say that:

> [U]ntil you know that you have been paid out, there's still the anticipation and there's still that nice suspense in the air ... but I do remember the next morning feeling quite deflated, we had got the prize which was great, but because it was over, the game was over, I felt a bit, deflated. So yes, the buzz was every bit as good as the prize, if not more.

Reflection and Re-Imaginings

The interview and workshop with Allison not only reveals the experience of risk from the perspective of one former career criminal but this glimpse into his life course through narrative tells so much more and in so doing it re-opens and reinforces an array of research, questions and possibilities. It appears that for Allison at least, risk is part and parcel of career criminality in the assessment and avoidance of risk, the implementation of risk-avoidance strategies and in the embracing and enjoyment of risk. The latter has been embodied and analysed by cultural criminologists and by sociologists such as Katz (1988). The former is encapsulated in the impact of new penology on criminology and state actors' preoccupation with risk identification and management and risk-focused intervention (O'Malley, 2010). But what can be learnt and re-learnt through Allison's criminal career and his relationship with risk and the criminal justice system?

Had Allison been identified as a risk at the onset of his criminal career what, if any, early intervention or risk-focused intervention would have prevented him from entering a life of crime? Could any measures reduce the pleasurable side of risk? Current punitive intervention still relies heavily on incarceration as a penal practice. Allison experienced prisons for children and adults as schools and universities in crime and they did nothing to stop him from, nor did they play any role in his desistance from a life of crime. Quite the opposite, it consolidated, sealed and bolstered his future career criminality. The criminal justice response to Allison as 'bad' and in need of punishment via incapacitation at best aided, and at worse 'caused' his shift from primary to secondary deviance. Labelling, stigmatisation, a self-fulfilling prophecy, age and the time spent in prison meant that Allison's crimes became more specialised. His desistence from crime owes nothing to criminal justice interventions. Allison's abandonment of the commission of crime is a combination of serendipity and his familial relationships at a particular point in time. Significantly, Allison is not a different person, he has not been corrected or rehabilitated and his personal and professional moral code as an investigative journalist is not that dissimilar to when he was a career criminal. He has also not turned his back on crime, and criminal investigations of a journalistic and campaign nature have replaced the pleasurable aspect of risk in the commission of crime – although not entirely as he still misses that "special buzz".

There may be a place for understanding the role of risk as appealing and exciting in responses to crime but risk identification, management and risk-driven responses are arguably futile and possibly counterproductive. One certain conclusion is that in this instance (as in thousands of other instances as research both official and alternative testify) prison did not work. The authors contend that an individual cannot be punished, into being 'good' or no longer at risk of committing a crime. Therefore criminal justice responses to offenders, especially child offenders, whatever risk they pose need to be reimagined. Alternative punishments or responses do not have to be sought – they exist (Parliamentary Office of Science and Technology, 2008; Make Justice Work, 2011) – but there is not the political will to make such measures the primary penal practice rather than cast to the margins. Underpinning recent concerns with risk and risky populations is the politicisation of crime and criminal justice (Garland, 2001). If there is resistance to taking the politics out of crime – then political courage is needed to resist the new penological turn and the reliance on the secure estate to deal with what are overwhelmingly troubled and vulnerable children and adults (see the work of Allison, http://www.guardian.co.uk/profile/ericallison and The Prison Reform Trust, 2012). Finally the biggest risks are: one, the failure to act on findings that have been well documented within and without critical criminology with regard to the failings of the criminal justice system and the secure estate in particular. Two, there is the continued risk of doing more harm to offenders, which produces detrimental results for society and ultimately victims.

References

Allison, E. (2008, 25 January). Research interview conducted with K. Corteen.

Allison, E. (2012a, September 5). The scandal of seriously ill prisoners denied basic healthcare. *The Guardian*. Retrieved from http://www.guardian.co.uk

Allison, E. (2012b, April 13). A true horror story: the abuse of teenage boys in a detention centre. *The Guardian*. Retrieved from http://www.guardian.co.uk

Allison, E. (2012c, October 30). The prison service's treatment of women is shameful. *The Guardian*. Retrieved from http://www.guardian.co.uk

Allison, E. (2013, February 8). Appeal court orders release of severely disabled prisoner. *The Guardian*. Retrieved from http://www.guardian.co.uk

Beck, B. (1992). *Risk society: Towards a new modernity*. London, United Kingdom: Sage.

Bell, E. (2010). The intensification of punishment from Thatcher to Blair: From conservative authoritarianism to punitive interventionism. Retrieved from: http://cle.ens-lyon.fr/anglais/the-intensification-of-punishment-from-thatcher-to-blair-from-conservative-authoritarianism-to-punitive-interventionism-90656.kjsp?RH=CDL_INF010000

Blumstein, A., Cohen, J., Roth, J. A., & Visher, A. (1986). Executive summary. In A. Blumstein, J. Cohen, J. A. Roth, & C. A. Visher (Eds.), *Criminal careers and 'career criminals', Volume 1*. Washington, DC: United States: National Academy Press. Retrieved from http://www.nap.edu/catlog/ 922.html

Corteen, K., & Allison, E. (2012). Career criminality: A risky business. *Earning a crust: Deconstructing work, wealth and opportunity conference*. Department of Social Studies and Counselling, University of Chester, 6 March 2012.

DeLisi, M. (2005). *Career criminals and society*. London, United Kingdom: Sage.

Farrall, S., & Calverley, A. (2006). *Understanding desistance from crime: Theoretical directions in resettlement and rehabilitation*. Maidenhead, United Kingdom: Open University Press.

Farrall, S., Bottoms, A., & Shapland, J. (2010). Social structures and desistance from crime. *European Journal of Criminology*, 7(6), 546–570.

Farrall, S., Sharpe, G., Hunter, B., & Calverley, A. (2011). Theorizing structural and individual-level processes in desistance and persistence: Outlining an integrated perspective. *Australian & New Zealand Journal of Criminology, 44*(2), 218-234.

Farrington, D. (1992). Criminal career research in the United Kingdom. *British Journal of Criminology, 32*(4), 521-536.

Farrington, D. P. (2003). *What has been learned from self-reports about criminal careers and the causes of offending*. London, United Kingdom: Home Office.

Feeley, M., & Simon, J. (1992). The new penology: notes on the emerging strategy of corrections and its implications. *Criminology, 30*, 449-474.

Ferrell, J. (1995). Culture, crime and cultural criminology. *Journal of Criminal Justice and Popular Culture, 3*(2), 25-42.

Ferrell, J. (2005). The only possible adventure: edgework and anarchy. In S. Lyng (Ed.), *Edgework: The sociology of risk-taking* (pp. 75-88). Abingdon, United Kingdom: Routledge.

Ferrell, J., Hayward, K., Morrison, W., & Presdee, M. (Eds.). (2004). *Cultural criminology unleashed*. London, United Kingdom: Glasshouse Press.

Ferrell, J., Hayward, K., & Young, J. (2008). *Cultural criminology*. London, United Kingdom: Sage.

Ferrell, J., Milovanovic, D., & Lyng, S. (2001). Edgework, media practices, and the elongation of meaning. *Theoretical Criminology, 5*(2), 177-202.

Ferrell, J., & Saunders, C. R. (Eds.). (1995). *Cultural criminology*. Boston, MA: Northeastern University Press.

Garland, D. (1996). The limits of the sovereign state: strategies of crime control in contemporary society. *British Journal of Criminology, 36*, 445-471.

Garland, D. (2001). *The culture of control*. Oxford, United Kingdom: Oxford University Press.

Giddens, A. (1999). Risk and responsibility. *The Modern Law Review, 62*(1), 1–10.

Hebdige, D. (1979). *Subculture: The meaning of style*. London, United Kingdom: Routledge.

Jameson, N., & Allison, E. (1995). *Strangeways 1990: A serious disturbance*. London, United Kingdom: Larkin Publications.

Jewkes, Y. (2011). *Media and crime*. (2nd ed.). London, United Kingdom, Sage.

Katz, J. (1988). *The seductions of crime*. New York, NY: Basic Books.

Lyng, S. (1990). *Edgework*. New York, NY: Routledge.

Lyng, S. (2004). Crime, edgework and corporeal transaction. *Theoretical Criminology, 8*(3), 359–375.

Lyng, S. (2005). Edgework and the risk-taking experience. In S. Lyng (Ed.). *Edgework: The sociology of risk-taking* (pp. 3–16). Abingdon, United Kingdom: Routledge.

Make Justice Work, (2011). *Community or custody? Which works best? A national inquiry*. Retrieved from http://communityorcustody.com/National%20Enquiry%20-%20Final%20Report.pdf

O'Malley, P. (2010). *Crime and risk*. London, United Kingdom: Sage.

Parliamentary Office of Science and Technology (2008). *Alternatives to custodial sentencing: May, Number 208*. Parliamentary Office of Science and Technology. Retrieved from http://oro.open.ac.uk/19037/1/pdf22.pdf

Prison Reform Trust. (2012). *Bromley briefings prison factfile: November*. London, United Kingdom: Prison Reform Trust.

Risley, S. (2006). 'The sociology of security: Sociological approaches to contemporary and historical securitization'. Paper presented at the annual meeting of the American Sociological Association, Montreal, Quebec, Canada, 10 August. Retrieved from http://www.allacademic.com/meta/p105192_index.html

Sim, J. (2009). *Punishment and prisons: Power and the carceral state*. London, United Kingdom: Sage.

Slingeneyer, T. (2007). The new penology: A grid for analyzing the transformation of penal discourses, techniques and objectives. *The New International Journal of Criminology, 4*. Retrieved from http://champpenal.revues.org/7798

Soothill, K., Fitzpatrick, C., & Frances, B. (2009). *Understanding criminal careers*. Cullompton, United Kingdom: Willan.

CHAPTER 6

TRANSFORMATIVE LEARNING EXPERIENCES IN 'HARD TO REACH' YOUNG ADULT LEARNERS' INITIAL ENGAGEMENT IN LEARNING

Paul Wagg

This chapter discusses transformative learning experiences in 'hard to reach' young adult learners' initial engagement in learning, and the reciprocity that transformative learning may have with the learning processes of reflective thinking, critical thinking and self-efficacy. Consideration is given to the social locus of the 'hard to reach' learner in a modern democratic society, to the central notions of educational inclusion and exclusion, and to the advantages of inclusion and the disadvantages of exclusion, both at an individual micro level and also in terms of the greater macro context of society. At the individual level it incorporates the rights of individuals to fair and equal opportunities; at the societal level it is concerned with increased social cohesion and the creation of a society to which people feel they belong and within which they are valued. It has a focus on educational inclusivity, and the relationship of this to learning policy in the United Kingdom. This is discussed against a background of conflicting economic and social ideologies, which shape the purpose and intent of education. The current trend in learning policy is one that emphasises the development of skills to meet the demands of a competitive global economy against the development of learning for personal development and expansion of critical consciousness, external to an economic paradigm. The conclusions of this chapter are based upon qualitative research completed by the author in 2013, in which 'hard to reach' young adult learners not in education, employment or training (NEETs), who attended a 12-week Prince's Trust course at a college of Further Education, and their course tutors, were interviewed regarding the student learning experience.

Learning is viewed by the National Institute of Adult and Continuing Education (NIACE) (2000) as a means for experiencing personal development with regard to such qualities as self-esteem, confidence and identity. Exclusion from education has previously been understood against a backcloth of long-standing inequalities in the distribution of wealth and power, brought about and reinforced by the inequalities of economic and class systems. The root cause of social exclusion according to NIACE (2000) is poverty. How poverty is addressed through government policy varies according to where prevailing political ideology considers the root causes of poverty to lie. From an educational perspective this then determines whether the emphasis in education policy is given to economic or social concerns and aspirations. Wilson and Train (2006) point out that whilst education is not the sole means of effecting an inclusive, equal, fair and cohesive society, it may through enabling the development of an informed awareness and skills, contribute considerably to developing such a society within which individuals develop and are active participants. Social inclusion is concerned with engaging individuals and groups more fully in society and educational inclusion is considered as an important component in the fostering of an inclusive society (Department of Health, 2003). The fostering of social inclusion through education is viewed by Balatti, Black, and Falk, (2009) as being more than just the responsibility of the education system, and also involving collective partnership across government sectors, community groups and industry. These authors consider the notion that a new perspective on education has been opened up which enables stakeholder partnerships to have a collective, collaborative responsibility to deliver education into social spaces, thus fostering the development of networks and consequently, of social capital and social inclusion. They state, "There seems to be a belief that providing education and training as part of wider efforts to increase social inclusion is a collective responsibility and ultimately in the best interests of industry and community" (Balatti et al., 2009, p. 38).

The concept of educational inclusion can be set within a wider social context and includes the notion of a cohesive society. The effect of educational inclusion goes beyond the classroom; it may be viewed as a concern to promote the right to equal opportunity as a fundamental value of a fair and just society. In addressing the inequalities of access to participation in education suffered by socially excluded learners of all ages, this concern is mindful of exclusion due to differences, such as minority religious and ethnic groups, asylum seekers, travellers, teenage mothers, gender and sexual orientation (Office for Standards in Education, Children's Services and Skills (OFSTED), 2002).

An understanding of the processes leading to inequality of opportunity for individuals and groups is captured by the notion of what Ball (2003) refers to as 'class strategies'. These class strategies operate as a means to defend, hold and improve individual class position in society. Class strategies, according to Preston (2004), may involve the civic inclusion of favoured groups and the civic exclusion of others who are members of different social groups. These strategies incorporate more than just economic, income or occupational senses of class, but may consist of a combination of such categories as race and gender. Such combinations may then be a means of identifying those who 'belong' and those who do not, those who are included and those who are not. The excluded may then become 'hard to reach' through having a diminished sense of belonging to, or involvement in, a wider society. Approaches towards inclusion in learning are primarily concerned with redressing this imbalance and fostering equal opportunity.

As indicated by Brackertz and Meredyth (2008), the term 'hard to reach' can be used to refer to sections of the community that are difficult to involve in public participation, be it educational or civic participation. As a descriptive term, it offers a basis from which to consider the empowerment of a process of equality and social justice through inclusivity in education. The term itself is difficult both to define and to operationalise; seemingly this difficulty is reflected in an apparently increasing list of persons who fall into this category. 'Hard to reach' may include sections of or individual members of minority groups, such as minority ethnic people, gays and lesbians, or homeless people, who meet with barriers to engaging in learning through the view that society has of them being 'other', or indeed that a perception of being other is one that they hold of themselves. The construct of other is considered by Beauvoir (1946) to be as primordial as consciousness itself, so that a group having its own identity has an inherent tendency to set up any other group as 'other'. This involves a power dynamic which produces a perception of difference, invoking dualistic notions such as superior/inferior, of value/of no value, strange/familiar, and threatening/non-threatening. These dichotomies form the basis for inclusion and exclusion. The empowerment through education of members of society, deemed as on the margins, or deemed as 'other', can conceivably enable their fuller participation in society, a fuller belonging and a fuller realisation of individual potential; consequently the potential for both social cohesion and economic competitiveness is increased.

Lifelong Learning Policy in the United Kingdom
Initially the promotion of lifelong learning formed a significant element of New Labour's Social Reform Programme. Arising from the Social Exclusion Report (Social Exclusion Unit, 1998), it proffered, as a part of the National Strategy for Neighbourhood Renewal, a combination of initiatives to address perceived deficiencies in adult basic skills. Together with a commitment to lifelong learning and the Aimhigher programme it seemed to indicate a renewed energy for the re-introduction of access programmes (Diamond, 2008). The Aimhigher excellence programme was initially set up in 2001 (West, Hind, Pennel, Emmerson, Frayne, McNally, & Silva, 2006) as a series of national initiatives. Its intention was to enable an inclusivity of more young people from under-represented groups and backgrounds in access to higher education (McCaig, Bowers-Brown, Stevens, & Harvey, 2006). Whilst the primary group was 13–19-year-olds, it was also intended to widen participation to adults under 30 years of age (DfES, 2003). It was accompanied by a shift from the previous emphasis on organisational reform, to a view that change could be effected through four key aims (West et al., 2006):

1. To develop strong ties and partnerships between Further Education, local communities and employers.
2. To increase funding to higher education institutions to reach out to more young people.
3. To provide clear information and improved marketing of the route to higher education.
4. To pilot new forms of financial help to young people.

Potentially the first aim may have brought about a sense of locality and community which would have addressed concerns regarding social cohesion, but according to Diamond (2008) whilst community education has developed at new sites, funding for Further Education colleges and community learning initiatives has diminished. One consequence, as contended by Shaw (2008), is a process of marginalisation of adult education, which whilst engaging disadvantaged groups has become disadvantaged itself. This to some extent is a dislocation between on the one hand, widening participation and access to higher education, and on the other, adult learning and neighbourhood renewal. Diamond (2008) argues that both adult education through FE colleges, and as part of regeneration at community education sites, can coexist whilst having separate learning locations.

Vickers (2008) considers that the New Labour Government presumed that economically driven education for adults would, of itself, foster inclusion. As Vickers further points out, given this belief it therefore seems unlikely that government policy would give credence to the notion of funding social purpose education purely for its inherent value. Social purpose education is viewed by Fieldhouse (1992) as being that education which is designed to improve justice, equality and democracy and wherein education is considered as central to the struggle for social change. The contrasting view of education for economic purpose views education policy from a framework of neoliberalism (Jackson, 2007); it focuses attention solely on education as being the transfer of knowledge for the purpose of productivity. Jackson considers this focus to be education for the purpose of training and as such, to be a diminishing of education from the traditional values of learning. Jackson (2007) further invokes the notion of 'diaspora' to describe the scattering and exiling of these values which, Johnston (1999) considers, provide more potential for adult education to equip individuals and groups with the knowledge to challenge inequalities in society in order to make a world which is just and fair. Education for training with its emphasis on technical knowledge and skills training is concerned with adaptation to a global market (Jackson, 2010). Its emphasis on mere technique is considered by Freire (2004) as impoverished and emptied of those dreams which originally inspired a fight for social equality and that were the initial aspirations of a liberal adult education.

There is also a diminishing of the parameters of what passes for lifelong learning, so that as the influence of a hegemonic economic discourse becomes dominant in education, it presents a narrowed focus with an inherent intolerance which excludes, reduces and fragments the ideals, values and norms of lifelong learning and education for social purpose. The inference from the dominant neoliberal market discourse is that within its parameters exists the norm, the utopia, the ideal, in which a value is placed only on that learning which directly serves its purpose. Without those parameters exists the 'other' and what is of no value, learning that does not serve its purpose. The experience of being exiled is experienced by those who adhere to the exiled values; in terms of education it is experienced by those educationalists for whom learning encompasses a more holistic vision of human beings and their location in society, above and beyond an economic utility.

A solely economic education discourse may create new, whilst perpetuating existing, barriers to learning. Such an education may be one that does not take cognisance of what Wilson and Train (2006) refer to as "the less tangible outcomes of the impact of adult basic education" (p. 1), the dismissal of which may result in an impoverished learning experience.

Transformative Learning Experiences

Economically driven education policy, whilst preparing a workforce fit for purpose in a global economy, may also contribute a negative effect in part, on adult learning through a devaluing of that learning which makes an inherent social contribution.

The initial promotion of lifelong learning which formed a significant element of New Labour's social aspects of learning (for example, learning for social purpose, which in itself does not reflect the norms and values of an economic paradigm), was however followed by an increasing trend towards greater economically driven education. The current Conservative-Liberal Democrat Coalition Government, maintains a considerable focus on education and training for the purpose of national economic competitiveness, as apparent in their policy document 'Rigour and Responsiveness in Skills', jointly produced by the Department of Business, Innovation and Skills and the Department of Education (2013). A central thrust of this policy is to remove bureaucratic obstacles that have been argued to constrain the response of colleges to meet the needs of employers. A statement is made in the document which reflects the tone of its focus: "if a qualification is not a passport to a job or a level of higher qualification it has no purpose" (p. 5), evoking a response from The National Institute of Adult Continuing Education (NIACE, 2013) that the statement is "wrong, or at best an over-simplistic interpretation of the research" (p. 4). NIACE further points out that the document gives no consideration to the contribution that knowledge acquisition through lifelong learning may make to the development of human potential and to social and community cohesion. NIACE's contention being that education should have a fuller and more inclusive vision than labour-market learning. An outcome of the present government's policy may be a low priority being placed on those groups who find themselves unable to adapt to the prevailing economic skill values, thus increasing the marginalisation of individuals and sections of society. It seems inevitable that in any competitive environment not everyone can be winners in economic terms. It appears of concern therefore that the hegemony of an economic discourse may be limited in its capacity to be inclusive of those deemed to have little to contribute to increasing UK economic competitiveness. As a consequence of an emphasis on competitiveness, education policy is likely to be dictated by the need for economic utility, rather than by that for human personal and social growth.

The philosopher and educational reformer John Dewey considered that a diminishing of democracy occurs when the aims of education are disproportionately dictated from outside (Dewey, 1916). When this occurs, as in the current economic hegemony in learning discourse, this may not, as indicated by Carneiro, Dearden, and Vignoles (2010), necessarily result in a more economically productive person, and may merely be a use of education as an expensive sorting device, to enable employers to identify apparently more able individuals. Dewey (1916) further contends that in such a context the aims of learners do not arise from the free growth of their own experiencing, but are the external aims of others, so that their learning serves the ulterior aims of others rather than serving their own aims. There appears in the United Kingdom to be a move towards a more functional role for adult education with no space for what Mayo and Thompson (1995) refer to as "transformative learning processes" (p. 144), in which learners are involved in reflecting upon their own assumptions and beliefs as part of the transformative learning process (Mezirow, 1991). According to Christie (2009), when paradigms or a single paradigm dominate, at either the individual, group, institutional or state level, it is probably time to begin to question, if not subvert, them. Christie suggests that the best way to do this is to train people to think for themselves.

A Theoretical Framework
The transformative learning theory of Mezirow (2010) provides a central perspective from which previous 'hard to reach' adult learners' engagement in learning can be viewed. Other learning perspectives will be considered together as forming a quadratic theoretical framework with transformative learning theory. These include Bandura's (1986) self-efficacy theory, reflective thinking theory (Dewey, 1933), and the more definitive theory of critical thinking (Glaser, 1941); this last theory arose from Dewey's theory of reflective thinking and has been referred to as the cornerstone of the critical thinking movement by Yildrim and Ozkahraman (2011). The intention is that from a consideration of the role that these learning approaches have in the learning process, a more extensive understanding and perspective on learner transformation can be developed. The development of an extended understanding, according to Mezirow (1997), involves an individual changing their frame of reference regarding their assumptions and beliefs, and putting into action plans which enable new perspectives on how they perceive the world and their relationship to it. These four approaches share a common notion of potential shifts in self-perspective leading to self-improvement as a result of the development of what Richard Paul describes as an ability to think about your thinking, while you are thinking (Paul, 1993).

Transformative Learning Theory
Mezirow (2000, 2010) identifies ten stages of the learning process which together constitute the transformative learning

experience. The progress of the learner through these stages is one that potentially takes them through a process of critical thinking about their own context and location in terms of such things as attitude and belief. These stages are identified as:

1. An awareness of discontent.
2. A self-examination accompanied by feelings of fear, guilt and shame.
3. A critical assessment of assumptions.
4. A recognition of one's discontent, a realisation that others have negotiated a similar change and the experience of the process of transformation, are shared through discussion.
5. Exploration of new roles and relationships.
6. Planning a course of action.
7. Acquiring knowledge and skills for implementing one's plans.
8. Provisional trying of new roles and ways of being.
9. Building up competence and self-confidence.
10. A reintegration into one's life on the basis of conditions dictated by one's new perspective.

Taylor (2008) draws attention to the transformative learning process as taking place within a pre-existing frame of reference consisting of structures of assumptions and expectations that influence an individual's personal perspective and tacit understanding. These assumptions thereby influence their thinking, beliefs and actions. Together, the revision of a frame of reference and reflection on experience achieve a transformation in the individual's internal frames of reference. The main aim of transformative learning according to Christie (2009), and also the most difficult step, is to change both any invalid assumptions through which an individual interprets the world, and the behaviour that is based on them.

Transformative Learning Experiences

Reflective thinking and critical thinking
The concepts of critical thinking and reflective thinking are frequently used synonymously. According to Halpern (1996), critical thinking is specific and goal-directed towards problem solving and intended outcomes. Reflective thinking is an element of the critical thinking process and is the attempt to understand and analyse what has happened; it looks at the knowledge and belief basis of experience and includes attempts to make sense of the implications and legitimacy of such knowledge and beliefs (Dewey, 1933). Whilst critical thinking and reflective thinking are different, they are together necessary for the completion of an ongoing process of effective learning. As such, reflective thinking may be perhaps considered as informing critical thinking; the two are intricately and reciprocally woven together so that it is difficult to assert one without maintaining cognisance of the implications for the other.

Self-Efficacy
Bandura's (1986) triadic theory of reciprocal causation (Figure 1) considers that environment causes behaviour but that behaviour also causes environment, and suggests a triadic relationship between three factors argued to contribute to an individual's sense of self-efficacy:

    A. Personal factors comprised of experiences of performance, cognitions, affect and biological events.
    B. Behaviour.
    C. Environmental influences.

Self-efficacy refers to an individual's beliefs about his/her capabilities to succeed or perform well at specific tasks (Bandura, 1986; Schunk, 2000). Such self-belief also incorporates a belief in an ability to mobilise personal cognitive resources to meet and master the presenting situation. It also has an inherent predictive component of how much energy will be applied to completing the task (Mitchell, Hopper, Daniels, George-Falvy, & James, 1994). The idea that arises from this is that self-efficacy beliefs may enable an individual to exercise a measure of control over their thoughts, feelings and actions, and what an individual thinks, believes and feels affects how they will perform or behave. Bandura's (1986) social cognitive theory has this triadic reciprocal causation model as the central framework for understanding, predicting and changing behaviour. This model emphasises the role played by cognition in human awareness and the importance of a capacity for reflective thinking. The component of reflective thinking suggests reciprocity with similar aspects of the process of transformative learning, since as considered by Taylor (2008), reflection on experience is essential to a transformative learning process in which assumptions and beliefs are challenged leading to changes in behaviour.

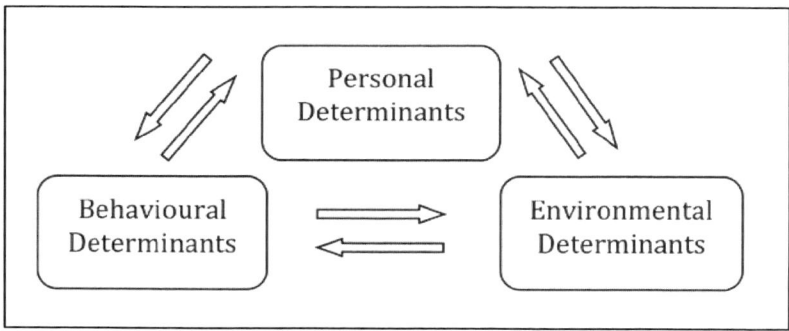

Figure 1: Triadic Reciprocal Causation (adapted from Bandura, 1986 p. 24).

Transformative Learning in the Research Context
A core question addressed by this research was: 'If transformative learning is occurring, does the experience have reciprocity with processes of critical thinking, reflective thinking and self-efficacy?'

Evidence accrued from student experience in this research indicated initially that transformative learning had taken place in students and that there was justification to suggest that the process has some reciprocity with self-efficacy, reflective thinking and critical thinking. However, what unfolded from a continued consideration was an overall sense that the theory of transformative learning itself becomes more and more limited as a means to understanding the complexities of learning. This was evident to such an extent that the theory began to be inconsistent with the realities of the student experience (within the learning context). What appeared to be indications of reciprocity became uncertain, since the number of changes occurring that might be identified as a transformative learning process appeared to be ongoing at different stages – both pre-engagement and post-engagement in learning.

The evidence indicated that whilst reflection on dissatisfaction occurred pre-engagement in learning for adult 'hard to reach' learners, students expressed a pre-engagement in learning dissatisfaction in unique ways. These included such things as a sense of feeling that life was meaningless and without a definitive time structure as if nothing mattered in life and nothing happened; or an experiencing of themselves as being unable to engage meaningfully in life and having no response to effectively change this uncomfortable experiencing, as illustrated by the following students' comments:

> It got to the point where I was not even bothering to go have a shower, have a shave, there was no purpose. I use to drink myself asleep and get up at two o'clock in the afternoon. (Rick, Entry Interview)

Another student described the dissatisfaction in the following way:

> It was horrible like, and I was just getting bored with nothing really to do. (Peter, Entry Interview)

One student reported:

> I have had no meaning in life, like an empty body. If you know what I mean? (Annabel, Entry Interview)

and provided a further image of the sense of emptiness:

> Just a shell. (Annabel, Entry Interview)

However, it was also evident from the student's experiencing, that a motivating factor that stimulates an impetus for enquiry into learning is a gathering or clustering of memories of previous experiences of self-efficacy. This impetus is not primarily a reflection on discontent, but contains elements of an awareness of unfulfilled potential. This suggests that reflective thinking, pre-engagement in learning, is not confined to a focus on feelings of discontent or dissatisfaction as the single initial primary process of transformative learning. This is the case as the discontent may be a necessary, but not a sufficient factor, in the initial stage. For example, one student stated:

> I could have done something with myself. I have wasted opportunity (Annabel, Entry Interview)

Some of the students held the following beliefs in the possession of personal qualities prior to the course:

> Well I've always known that I've been reasonably intelligent, do you know what I mean? (Stewart, Exit Interview)

> I knew I was a people's person. I knew I would be good at all that working for the NHS and all that. (Lauren, Exit Interview)

It is at this pre-engagement in learning phase that it becomes apparent that a possible shift, change or transformation has occurred prior to engagement in learning and that this is shortly followed by another process of transformative learning after engagement. Consequently, within the context of this research, transformative learning theory begins to be unwieldy and strained in its usefulness in enabling an understanding of the complexity of the learning processes taking place. There is no clear indication of when a transformative learning process begins or ends, or whether there may be more than one transformative learning process in operation. Indeed it is conceivable that a transformative process in itself can be occurring at any one moment, be at a different stage of transformation, and be of a different, unrelated transformative process to any other that may be taking place. It is therefore not clear whether such processes may be related, or whether they are linear and singularly follow their own separate sequence of transformative learning stages as proposed by Mezirow (2010).

There was evidence for reciprocity between self-efficacy and some of the stages of transformative learning, in particular where an emphasis on reflective thinking and critical thinking was indicated. However, the case for the completion of a transformative learning process rests ultimately on evidencing a critical evaluation of previous assumptions, leading students to changes in perspectives. That learning and change occurred is apparent, but that this was transformative learning, and led to changes in perspective, is more obscure. Pre-engagement in learning, students may for example have established assumptions arising from earlier adverse learning and life experiences of being rejected or excluded. This may be as a consequence of having for example a criminal record or an alcohol addiction. These are not necessarily inaccurate assumptions or interpretations on their part, but may be realistic views, formed on the basis of what past real experience, as opposed to imagined or assumed experience, of exclusion has yielded. So their fears of rejection that have prevented their engagement in learning may well be the result of effective reflective thinking and critical thinking processes.

Within the context of this study, the changes that students experience as a result of engaging in learning do not readily equate to a transformative experience, but rather to an informative expansion of understanding; the students' previous assumptions that they will not be included within a learning context or educational setting, may still hold true and be borne out in some other life contexts. A consideration arose from this research that the change experienced by students may be conformist rather than transformative, which resonates with Newman's (2012) notion that what we interpret as the development of personal agency as a result of transformative learning, may only be responses to trends, social conditioning and pressures within the context of the day. It is the notion of contexts that has a central place in regarding what contributes to enabling the learning to take place. The indications are that the learning took place within a climate of acceptance created by the tutors, which effectively undermined the unhelpful assumptions that students may have had about themselves and how tutors might interact with them. The previously held assumptions of the students, that could have potentially adversely shaped the learning experience into one of a self-fulfilling prophecy, were displaced largely by the tutor attitudes, which conveyed an acceptance, a valuing of, and a belief in the student's capacity to succeed. It was the sustaining of such an attitude of acceptance by the tutors that was the consistent backdrop to the fostering of quality learning experiences, which in turn sustained the previous 'hard to reach' learners in their learning process, through the creating of a safe and secure environment, one within which learners risked performing, experimenting and learning with minimisation of concerns of being adversely judged. Hence the transformation is not in the learners but in the learning climate to which they are exposed. There appears a case therefore for investigating the possibility of reciprocity between tutor acceptance and student self-efficacy, and for identifying what human elements constitute an effective learning environment for 'hard to reach' adult learners and what will sustain them in learning. A sense of a non-judgemental climate is indicated in the following statement made by a student:

> You are just comfortable around them. They [The tutors] help because they don't judge you. They said the first day you are in here we don't know your background why you act the way you do. So we [do not] ... judge you as a person. (Peter, Entry Interview)

The tutor interviews evidenced also a non-judgemental attitude of acceptance that fostered an encouraging learning climate. As one tutor, Matt, put it:

> Someone might aspire to be a street performer but as long as that is something they aspire to be and they want to do and

that's going to bring them some money in at fairs and carnivals then that's something they should be supported in. That's what I believe personally and maybe it's that attitude that they don't necessarily get from the parents. Parents always want what's best for the young people, they don't necessarily want what's right for them if that makes any sense. (Matt)

A more complex tapestry of the learning processes involved is revealed that cannot be accounted for by transformative learning, so that transformative learning theory appears limited at its best and of no consequence at its worst, in supporting an adequate understanding of the learning processes in the context of this research. Other processes, unacknowledged within the scope of transformative learning, cannot be readily excluded from a fuller understanding, but are important to recognise as contributing to an understanding of the learning process as a whole. These include a sense of unfulfilled potential, previous experiences of self-efficacy and a consistent climate of acceptance, which play a fundamental part in enabling learning processes of critical reflection, critical thinking and increasing perceived self-efficacy to develop.

However, with regard to transformative learning theory, as explained above, there is less indication that a process of learning has led to transformation, so the theory is not consistently substantiated within this research context. A process of transformation appears as too abstract to account for the complexity of the learning evidenced from the learners' experiences. There appears to be some possible points which allude to transformative learning having reciprocity with other accounts of learning as discussed here (reflective thinking, critical thinking and self-efficacy), but not to a degree that a conclusion of reciprocity can be justified in the face of the complexity that emerged. What transformative learning theory has to offer to understanding does not appear to go beyond a mirroring in some of its stages of these other accounts of learning. This could be misconstrued as reciprocal when it is not and reminiscent of an 'emperor's new clothes' experience, in that what initially appears to have substance has from a more considered perspective transparency that offers no material basis. If transformative learning is not actually taking place then there is no justification for arguing that it has made any contribution through reciprocity. It appears as too much of an overarching theory to encompass the intricacies of the learning process in light of what becomes apparent through closer scrutiny, for example, transformative learning at Stage 1 of Mezirow (2010) in anticipating that reflection on discontent is proposed as a dominant process, does not provide a full, adequate or sufficient picture of the subject of reflection that leads to motivation and movement towards learning.

Conclusions and Implications
The positive influence of a climate of acceptance in which previous 'hard to reach' young adult learners can flourish, has implications when considering that 'hard to reach' learners' past experiences of learning may not have been ones in which there was a nourishing relationship with tutors. In regard to the evidence from this research indicating the climate of acceptance that was fostered by tutors, it raises the notion that it may not be previous 'hard to reach' young adult learners that will change through a new process of learning, but that such changes may be as a result of a differing learning context. An element of this learning context may well be the tutor's communication to the learner of an attitude of acceptance, which in order to emphasise, I use the term 'particular acceptance' through which a sense of valuing the learner fosters the learner's experience of inclusivity. The

identification of acceptance as an important element in the tutor-learner relationship is one which has been earlier proposed by Rogers (1951) and Rogers and Freiberg (1993). Additionally, whilst the tutors' belief in the ability of the students to succeed is reminiscent of a Pygmalion effect (Rosenthal & Jacobson, 1968), a point to be considered is that such belief in students and high expectations of them, may be limited by the learning context, so that if training and employment are the central agenda then expectations will likely be limited to this. This infers that if there is no agenda for emancipatory conscientisation, by which a raising of critical awareness leads to emancipatory action (Friere, 2004), then there will be no emancipatory discourse, no expectation of emancipation and therefore no transformative learning.

A paucity or absence of such discourse in learning may have implications for democracy, so that the emperor's new clothes, that initially in this research were considered to be worn by the theory of transformative learning, may be metaphorically a wider indicator of a contemporary state of the illusion of the contemporary relationship between learning and democracy. A further consideration arising from this concerns the possible assumption, indeed possible illusion, that educators are themselves conscientiously emancipated, which alludes further to a possibility of degrees of emancipation, or degrees of an illusion of emancipation. This recalls the earlier notion of Dewey (1916) that a diminishing of democracy occurs when the aims of education are disproportionately dictated from outside, so that learning serves the ulterior aims of others; an implication may perhaps be drawn that if learning itself is not emancipated, then the notion that learning can emancipate is illusory.

The student's recollection of past memorable experiences and impressions of effective performance and self-efficacy at the pre-engagement stage of learning plays a part in motivating pre-engaged learners to contemplate engaging in learning. It seems therefore an important consideration for the continuity and retention of learners that this is acknowledged and affirmed early in the engagement in learning. This would be a recognition that previous 'hard to reach' young adult learners do not embark and engage on a course empty-handed, but already possess an ability to reflect, critique and act with confidence based on belief in their ability to succeed. At an individual micro-processing level, this might be achieved initially through a student identifying, prior to engagement in learning, their successful and unsuccessful past performances, identifying the skills and attitude that enabled this success or were needed to be successful, and the sharing and discussion of these experiences with others, so that the student as a whole, past and present, more fully occupies their space within the learning context. At the group level this would contribute to the learning experience by fostering group cohesion and belonging through shared experiences. Learners may well benefit from being introduced to the theories of reflective thinking, critical thinking and self-efficacy in a form which is understandable, so that they are provided with an informed knowledge baseline from which to develop a sense of value in their own capacity to develop the skills. On the basis of there being reciprocity of reflective thinking and critical thinking skills and perceived self-efficacy, there would seem to be advantages in encouraging the learner towards developing a disposition or inclination towards applying such skills.

Such a question may then begin to differentiate between what is meant by conforming and transforming, and whether education for previously 'hard to reach' young adult learners in any educational context, realistically embraces the concept of emancipatory conscientisation and provides fertile ground for such realisations, or indeed thwarts and undermines it, by offering no learning space, voice or discourse for the affirmation of such development. It further raises a consideration of the extent to which educators themselves are conscientiously emancipated within an education system which is driven by a dominant economic discourse.

References

Balatti, J., Black, S., & Falk, I. (2009). *A new social capital paradigm for adult literacy: Partnerships, policy and pedagogy.* Canberra, Australia: National Centre for Vocational Education Research (NCVER).

Ball, S. (2003). Class strategies and the education market. In T. Shuller, J. Preston, C. Hammond, A. Brassett-Grundy, & J. Bynner (Eds.), *The benefits of learning: The impact of education on health family life and social capital* (pp. 119–157). London, United Kingdom: Routledge Falmer.

Bandura, A. (1986). *Social foundations of thought and action: A social cognitive theory.* Englewood Cliffs, NJ: Prentice Hall.

Beauvoir, S. (1946). *The second sex.* London, United Kingdom: Penguin.

Brakertz, N., & Meredyth, D. (2008). *Social inclusion of the hard to reach.* Victoria, Australia: Swinburne Institute for Social Research, Swinburne University of Technology.

Carneiro, P., Dearden, L., & Vignoles, A. (Eds.). (2010). The economics of vocational education and training. *International Encyclopaedia of Education.* Oxford, United Kingdom: Elsevier.

Christie, M. (2009). *Transformative Learning in action.* Retrieved from http://upcommons.upc.edu/revistes/ bitstream/ 2099/7803/1/ale09-paper10.pdf

Department of Business, Innovation and Skills and the Department for Education. (2013). *Rigour and responsiveness in skills*. Retrieved from https://www.gov.uk/government/uploads/system/uploads/attachment_data/file/175554/13-960-rigour-and-responsiveness-in-skills.pdf

Department of Education and Skills (DfES). (2003). *The Future of Higher Education*. London, United Kingdom: Her Majesty's Stationery Office.

Department of Health. (2003). *National healthy school standard*. Retrieved from www.wiredforhealth.gov.uk

Dewey, J. (1916). *Democracy and education*. New York, NY: Free Press.

Dewey, J. (1933). *How we think: A restatement of the relation of reflective thinking and the educational process*. New York, NY: D. C. Heath.

Diamond, J. (2008). Access, widening participation and neighbourhood renewal: You can't have one without the other. *Widening Participation and Lifelong Learning, 10*(3), 6–13.

Fieldhouse, R. (1992). Tradition in British university adult education and the WEA. In C. Duke (Ed.), *Liberal and adult education: Perspectives and projects* (pp. 11–14). Warwick, United Kingdom: University of Warwick.

Freire, P. (2004). *Pedagogy of indignation*. Boulder, CO: Paradigm.

Glaser, E. M. (1941). *An experiment in the development of critical thinking*. Retrieved from http://www.criticalthinking.org/aboutCT/define_critical_thinking.cfm

Halpern, D. F. (1996). *Thought and knowledge: An introduction to critical thinking*. Mahwah, NJ: L. Erlbaum Associates.

Jackson, S. (2007). *In search of lifelong learning: politics, power and pedagogic challenges.* Retrieved from http://www.bbk.ac.uk/events/inaugural/jackson

Jackson, S. (2010). Learning through social spaces: Migrant women and lifelong learning in post-colonial London. *International Journal of Lifelong Education, 29*(2), 237–253.

Johnston, R. (1999). Adult learning for citizenship: Towards a reconstruction of social purpose tradition. *International Journal of Lifelong Education, 18*(3), 175–190.

Mayo, M., & Thompson, J. (Eds.). (1995). *Adult learning, critical intelligence and social change.* Leicester, United Kingdom: NIACE.

McCaig, C., Bowers-Brown, T., Stevens, A., & Harvey, L. (Higher Education Funding Council for England). (2006). *National evaluations of Aimhigher: Survey of higher education institutions, further education colleges and worked-based learning providers.* Retrieved from http://www.shu.ac.uk/research/ceir/sp-colin-ccaig.htm

Mezirow, J. (1991). *Transformative dimensions of adult learning.* San Francisco, CA: Jossey-Bass.

Mezirow, J. (1997). Transformative learning: Theory to practice. *Transformative Learning in Action; Insights from Practice. New Directions for Continuing Education, 74,* 5–12.

Mezirow, J. (2000). *Learning as transformation: Critical perspective on a theory in progress.* San Francisco, CA: Jossey-Bass.

Mezirow, J. (Ed.). (2010). *Transformative learning in practice: Insights from community, workplace and higher education.* San Francisco, CA: Jossey-Bass.

Mitchell, T. R., Hopper, H., Daniels, D., George-Falvy, J., & James, L. R. (1994). Predicting self-efficacy and performance during skill acquisition. *Journal of Applied Psychology, 79,* 506–517.

Newman, M. (2012). Calling transformative learning into question: Some mutinous thoughts. *Adult Education Quarterly, 62*(1), 36–55.

NIACE. (2013). *An early response to the government's paper on rigour and responsiveness in skills published by the Department of Business Innovation and Skills and the Department for Education.* Retrieved from http://www.niace.org.uk/sites/default/files/early_response_to_rigour_and_responsiveness_in_skills_1.pdf

NIACE. (2000). *Social exclusion: Briefing sheet 10.* Retrieved from http://archive.niace.org.uk/information/Briefing_sheets/Social_Exclusion. pdf (accessed 8 August 2012, no longer available).

OFSTED. (2002). *Evaluating educational inclusion: Guidance for inspectors and schools.* London, United Kingdom: Office for Standards in Education.

Paul, R. (1993). *Critical thinking: How to prepare students for a rapidly changing world.* Santa Rosa, CA: The Foundation for Critical Thinking.

Preston, J. (2004). A continuous effort of sociability: Learning and social capital in adult life. In T. Schuller, J. Preston, C. Hammond, A. Brassett-Grundy, & J. Bynner (Eds.), *The benefits of learning: The impact of education on health family life and social capital* (pp. 119–157). London, United Kingdom: Routledge Falmer.

Rogers, C. R. (1951). *Client-centered therapy.* Boston, MA: Houghton Mifflin.

Rogers, C. R., & Freiberg, H. J. (1993). *Freedom to Learn.* (3rd ed.). New York, NY: Merrill.

Rosenthal, R., & Jacobson, L. (1968). *Pygmalion in the classroom: Teacher expectation and pupils' intellectual development.* New York, NY: Irvington.

Schunk, D. H. (2000). *Learning theories: An educational perspective*. New Jersey, NJ: Prentice-Hall.

Shaw, J. (2008). The role of the voluntary sector in widening participation in higher education, *Journal of Voluntary Sector Research, 1*(1), 45–60.

Social Exclusion Unit. (1998). *Bringing Britain together: A national strategy for neighbourhood renewal: Cm. 4045*. London, United Kingdom: Social Exclusion Unit.

Taylor, E. (2008). Transformative learning theory. *New Directions for Adult and Continuing Education, 119*, 5–15.

Vickers, A. (2008). How the voluntary and community sector in the UK is advocating social purpose adult education in the face of globalisation. *Widening Participation and Lifelong Learning, 10*(1), 34–40.

West, A., Hind, A., Pennel, H., Emmerson, C., Frayne, C., McNally, S., & Silva, O. (Department for Education and Skills). (2006). *Evaluation of Aimhigher: Excellence challenge synthesis report: Surveys of opportunity bursary applicants and economic evaluation: Research Report 709*. Retrieved from http://dera.ioe.ac.uk/5888/

Wilson, K., & Train, B. (2006). The lifelong impact of lifelong learning; using qualitative evaluation to measure the less tangible outcomes of adult basic skills education. *Widening Participation and Lifelong Learning, 8*(1), 1–13.

Yildrim, B., & Ozkahraman, S. (2011). Critical thinking theory and nursing education. *International Journal of Humanities and Social Science, 1*(17), 176–185.

CHAPTER 7

WORK, RESILIENCE AND DISABILITY: 'CRIPPING' THE NORMS

Katherine Runswick-Cole and Dan Goodley

This chapter sets out to explore the interconnections between resilience, work and disability. We suggest that what disabled people tell us about work and resilience requires us to think again about work, disability and resilience in ways that challenge the often unspoken, but disabling, assumptions. This reflection is particularly important at a time when disabled people are excluded from the workplace while simultaneously facing cuts to out-of-work benefits. Our approach draws on an idea from the disabled people's movement that encourages us to 'crip the norms' (Goggin & Newell, 2004) in relation to resilience, work and disability.

Why Resilience?
This paper was from work carried out as part of a wider project conducted by the authors called: *Resilience in the lives of disabled people across the life course.*[1] The project, commissioned and funded by the UK disability charity, Scope, had the following aims:

- To explore what resilience means to disabled people at different stages across the life course.
- To explore how resilience, or a lack of it, has affected disabled people's ability to negotiate challenges and make the most of opportunities in their lives.

---

[1] For more information about the project visit: http://disability-resilience.posterous.com/

- To understand what works in building resilience amongst different groups of disabled people.
- To develop a toolkit for use by Scope's policy and services functions that outlines what Scope means by resilience, what does or doesn't work in supporting people to become resilient, and what we can do to build resilience in disabled people throughout the life course.

The research was carried out in four phases: a literature review; a life story phase in which we interviewed 43 disabled people (aged 5–83) and parents/carers of disabled children; a series of focus groups with disabled people of working age, parents/carers of disabled children and disabled young people and, finally, a Community of Practice phase (Lave & Wenger, 1991) which brought together disabled people and researchers to develop a toolkit for use with disabled people and in Scope's services

Given the current climate of economic restraint and a shrinking state which is inevitably impacting on the services and support disabled people can access (Runswick-Cole & Goodley, 2012), a study which focuses on understanding better what resilience is and how it develops in the lives of disabled people is timely. Throughout the study, disabled people's access to and engagement with work emerged as a key issue impacting on their sense of resilience.

Thinking About Resilience
In public discourse, resilience is perhaps most often described as the 'ability to bounce back' (Young, Green, & Rogers, 2008). There is an implicit assumption that a person must have experienced adversity, or overcome a significant barrier, in order to be described as resilient. This lay understanding of resilience is rooted in psychological approaches to resilience

which have characterised resilience as "a class of phenomena characterised by *good outcomes in spite of serious threats to adaptation of development*" (Masten, 2001, p. 228) or as "the positive pole of individual difference in people's response to stress and adversity" (Rutter, 1987 cited in Young et al., 2008, p. 41). Resilience is spoken of in relation to risk so that individuals who have not been exposed to risk but are judged to be 'living well' are not necessarily considered to be resilient whereas those that have been exposed to risk are (Masten, 2001).

Resilience and 'the Norm'
Resilience is often discussed in the context of developmental child psychology where resilient children are judged to have met 'normal' developmental milestones despite 'adversity'. As Masten (2001) says resilience is conceptualised as a commonplace phenomenon arising from "the every day magic of ordinary, *normative* human resources in the minds, brains and bodies of children, in their families and relationships and in their communities" (p. 235, emphasis added). However, as we argue elsewhere (Runswick-Cole & Goodley, 2013), concepts of resilience underpinned by 'norms' are clearly problematic when working with disabled people who are often viewed by medical professionals and by wider society in terms of their impairments and, by default, considered not to develop normally, nor to share personal characteristics with others without impairments. The presence of an impairment has, in and of itself, therefore excluded some disabled people from the category of 'resilient'.

Furthermore, by focusing on resilience as the product of an individual person's *normal* development and adaptation in the face of adversity, if a person fails to develop 'normally' or to adapt, there is an implicit assumption that the person is deficient in some way or is, perhaps, weak willed or lacking in 'inner strength'. People who fail to bounce back are seen to be wanting and often the responsibility for, or cause of this lack is seen as belonging to the individual themselves. The consequence of this is that individuals are then blamed for failing to possess the necessary personal characteristics needed to overcome adversity.

The Social Production of Resilience
Understandings of resilience as a personal characteristic of the individual have been challenged in a number of ways (Ungar, 2004, 2007). First, the direct causal relationship between the experience of risk and the emergence of resilience has been challenged. Traditional approaches to resilience research seem to suggest that there is a predictable relationship between risk and resilience so that when normal development is said to have occurred, despite the presence of adversity or risk, then the person is judged to be resilient. Interestingly, in the lives of disabled people, just as the presence of an impairment has been used to exclude disabled people from the category of resilience, as we saw above, the presence of an impairment can also mean that disabled people who meet cultural norms (or exceed them) are automatically seen to have overcome 'adversity' and to be resilient. This judgement is made despite the fact that not all people living with impairments regard their impairment as an experience of adversity. Indeed, many people with impairments wish to affirm their identity as a disabled person stressing the positive aspects of living with impairment (Swain & French, 2000). Clearly, what constitutes 'adversity' is contested. Furthermore, as Boyden (2001) points out, the relationship between adversity and resilience is unpredictable. As such, the relationship between risk and

resilience is chaotic, complex, relative, and context dependent (Boyden, 2001).

Crucially, for us here, Ungar (2007) has highlighted the global and cultural contexts in which resilience emerges. He points out that outcomes that might be seen as 'risk factors' in one context, such as leaving school early or becoming pregnant at a young age, are culturally embedded, reflecting the values of Global North countries (Ungar, 2007). Indeed, in a different context, the same outcomes might be seen as evidence of resilience, rather than risk-laden events. By paying attention to the cultural contexts in which resilience is said to emerge, Ungar (2007) reveals the ways in which resilience is socially created.

The Social Production of Disability
As we have described elsewhere (Runswick-Cole & Goodley, 2012), we are attracted to Ungar's (2004, 2007) arguments that resilience is socially produced because we are already convinced by accounts that reveal the social production of disability (Oliver, 1990). In 1981, Mike Oliver first used the phrase 'the social model of disability'. Oliver (2004) was trying to give people "a way of applying the idea that it was society not people with impairments that should be the target for professional intervention and practice" (pp. 18-19). In contrast to medical and individual models of disability, the social model of disability aims to move the focus away from the limitations of impaired bodies and to look instead at the difficulties caused for disabled people by disabling environments, barriers, attitudes and cultures. The aim, then, is to expose and remove barriers to disabled people's participation in all areas of life including: education, work environments, the benefits system, health and social services, housing, transport and the devaluing of disabled people in the

media (including newspapers, films, television and the internet) (Barnes, 2008).

By focusing on the social production of both resilience and disability, we can see that creating environments which support resilience can never simply be a matter of building individual capacity or family support, it must also be a case of challenging social, attitudinal and structural barriers which threaten resilience in the lives of disabled people (Young et al., 2008). Indeed, as Ungar tells us, there are "unique pathways to survival" (2005, p. 91) and that "[p]athways to resilience are a many splendored thing" (2007, p. 19). So, we need to be wary of approaches to resilience building that assume that only a rational, developing, striving individual who has done well against the odds can be judged to be resilient.

Networks of Resilience
We suggest that by taking a social constructionist approach to resilience and to disability it is possible to think about resilience in ways that are more enabling in disabled peoples' lives. Drawing influence from Ungar (2004, 2007), we have conceptualised resilience as a network made up of the following resources:

1. Material resources: Availability of financial, educational, medical, and employment opportunities or assistance, as well as access to food, clothing, and shelter to meet basic needs.
Exemplary question: How does access to employment opportunities and associated resources influence resilience?
2. Relationships: Relationships with significant others, peers, adults and children within one's family and community.

Exemplary question: How do relationships at work impact on a person's sense of resilience?
3. Identity: Personal and collective sense of self and purpose, self-appraisal of strengths and weaknesses, aspirations, beliefs and values, including spiritual and religious identification.
Exemplary question: How does a positive sense of self emerge through work?
4. Bodies: The influence of one's body – including impairment – in relationships with others.
Exemplary question: How does the body influence access to work and relationships at work?
5. Power and control: Experiences of caring for one's self and others; the ability to effect change in one's social and physical environment in order to access health, educational and community resources.
Exemplary question: To what extent do disabled people have power and control over their working lives?
6. Community participation: Taking part in one's community through a host of activities and engagements.
Exemplary question: How does work (or the lack of work) impact on meaningful community participation?
7. Social justice: Experiences related to finding a meaningful role in community and a sense of social equality.
Exemplary question: How do disabled people experience social equality at work?
8. Community cohesion: Balancing one's personal interests with a sense of responsibility to the greater good; feeling a part of something larger than one's self socially and spiritually.
Exemplary question: How does work impact on a sense of community cohesion in the lives of disabled people?

These resources are represented visually in Figure 1 (overleaf).

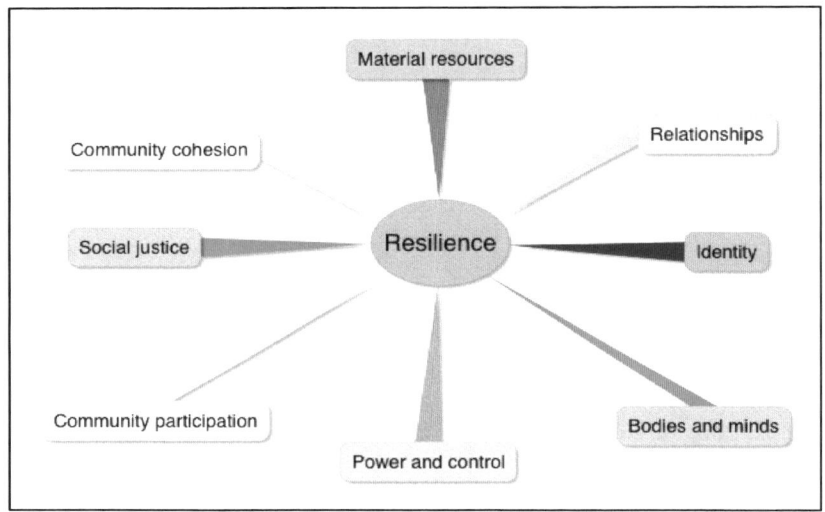

Figure 1: Network of resources (Runswick-Cole & Goodley, 2012).

These categories are not discrete entities, but are overlapping and interconnected.

The Economic and Cultural Context
This research was carried out in a time of economic recession in England. Clearly, the impact of economic cutbacks has fallen disproportionately on disabled people (Roulstone, 2011). This is in part because of the number of disabled people who are not in employment. The Office for Disability Issues (ODI) found that only 48% of disabled people are in employment compared with 78% of non-disabled people (ODI, 2011). The Children's Society (2011) found that four in ten disabled children live in poverty. Only 16% of mothers of disabled children have employment, compared to 61% of other mothers (Contact a Family, 2014).

The state benefit system is also undergoing radical change. The Coalition government has made a commitment to cut Disability Living Allowance (a tax-free benefit to help disabled people with extra costs) by 20% despite the lack of any evidence to suggest that there is this level of over-claiming of the allowance (Grant, 2011). The government will replace the Disability Living Allowance with a Personal Independence Payment in 2014, the impact of which is, as yet, unclear. In addition, the government has begun to migrate Incapacity Benefit claimants (Incapacity Benefit is an out-of-work payment for people who cannot work because of illness or disability) on to Employment Support Allowance or other moving-to-work benefits (Disability Alliance, 2011).

The new gateway to work benefits is the Work Capability Assessment (WCA) (Grant, 2011) a medical assessment based on a points system that determines who is 'ready for work' or not. The WCA represents an increasing focus on the *medical* aspects of disability, in contrast to *social* approaches. As a result, the WCA fails to attend to the social and practical factors that affect disabled people's lives. The outcome of the assessment is that disabled people are judged 'ready to work' or part of the 'support group' of people who are considered unable to work and will, therefore, be supported with benefits. It is expected that people with 'moderate learning disabilities', who may previously have been in receipt of Incapacity Benefit, will be placed in the 'ready to work' category and those with complex needs in the 'support group' that will receive benefits and not be required to seek work. The danger is that a medical assessment alone will be unable to take into account wider barriers to disabled people's access to work including affordable and accessible childcare, appropriate housing and confidence levels. As a result, a medical assessment will mean that some disabled people, who face considerable barriers to work, will be judged 'work ready', while other disabled people will, because of the identification of their complex needs, be judged 'unable to work' no matter what their circumstances. Successful appeals against the WCA stand at 40% (BMA, 2012). this suggests that the assessment is not working well for disabled people.

The government is committed to 'Work Choice' (formerly the Specialist Disability Employment Programme) (DWP, 2010), a small project limited to disabled people. Participants will be offered a set curriculum including: life skills, curriculum vitae development and interview training, but the number of disabled people who will access this programme will be small, an estimated 16,000 people over five years (http://www.goodaccessguide.co.uk/news/info. php?refnum =464).

Currently, the government also remains committed to the Access to Work scheme which funds equipment, or a support worker, for disabled people in the workplace. This scheme is being extended to supplement new supported internships for people with 'learning disabilities' which are also intended to move more disabled people into work (DWP, n.d.). However, the government has decided to close 27 factories employing disabled workers as part of Remploy. The government has promised to re-distribute the £320 million budget savings to improve employment services, and, although the move has been broadly welcomed by disabled people's organisations, the outcomes for the 1,700 redundant Remploy employees are expected to be poor (Butler, 2012).

Media coverage of Employment Support Allowance, Disability Living Allowance and the Motability Scheme (a scheme which provides transport for disabled people) have created an extremely negative public perception of the link between disability, welfare and work such that disabled people are seen as a drain on, rather than part of their communities (Roulstone, 2011). Disabled people are depicted as benefit scroungers and stories of fraudulent disability claims make the front pages of newspapers (*Daily Mail*, 2011). Indeed, Inclusion London (2011) found that the media coverage describing disabled people in sympathetic and deserving terms had fallen, whereas there was an increase in the number of articles focusing on disability benefit fraud.

In the following sections, we reflect on the interconnections between disability, work and resilience in the lives of disabled people, drawing on their accounts of their lives. The analysis of the accounts is guided by the network of resilience we identified above with the aim of exploring the interconnections between work, disability and resilience.

Material Resources

At a time of high unemployment, austerity measures, economic downturn and a government agenda to move people off benefits and into work, access to *material resources* is a key issue for disabled people of working age. The material foundations from which it is possible to bounce back are seriously under threat in the lives of disabled people. Increased competition for jobs and cultural anxiety about 'benefit scroungers' make the reality of work ever more difficult for disabled people. Indeed, for some disabled people, barriers to work seemed insurmountable:

> People don't help you [find a job] as well. ... You try to do voluntary work to try and get yourself better to try and help, but no one seems to want to give you a job. If they could help you with finding a job that you could cope with and you could manage and they had some understanding of your illness then it would be helpful but there is nothing like

that. We will take your money off you and no one will help you.

(Focus Group 1, Participant 3)

Parents/carers reported the attitudinal barriers that prevented them from working:

> If you've got an employer who knows that [someone has] got a disabled child, how flexible are they going to be? They need to be quite flexible and some employers aren't.
>
> (Focus Group 2, Participant 6)

Caring responsibilities were also identified as significant barriers to work:

> Even I wouldn't employ me, five doctors I see a month, who is going to employ me?
>
> (Focus Group 2, Participant 6)

The inaccessibility of paid work clearly impacts negatively on disabled people's resilience in terms of material resources, however, work represented far more than simply a material resource in people's lives, as we see below.

Identity and Community

For many disabled adults, work has a huge impact not only on financial resources, but also on sense of *identity* as someone who is valued and makes a contribution to the *community*. Matilda spoke of work as being a key part of her *identity*:

> I think for me as well one of the things that is important to me is to be needed and at work. Those times when I feel like my work is making a difference; it's almost as if I viewed resilience like a fuel that you put in your body; and it helps keep you going when times aren't so great. I can think back and say "I might be having a rubbish day at work today, but

remember how you felt when someone told you: 'Matilda this is really helpful it's really helped me with my work today'".

(Interviewee 1)

A parent told us:

> [without work] you lose your identity, work is more than just bringing money in. You just want a life like everybody else.
>
> (Focus Group 2, Participant 7)

Disabled people told us that work contributed to their sense of identity of someone who participated in and contributed to their communities.

Social Justice: Disability, Work and the Law
Crucially, disabled people reminded us of the ways in which legislation impacts on work opportunities:

> I'd be a Community Service Volunteer but about six weeks after my friends had gone to university, they told me that they couldn't take me because of my disability. This was pre-Disability Discrimination Act, of course.
>
> (Interviewee 2)

Interviewee 2's story is a timely reminder of the importance of protecting disabled people's right to work in law and the impact of legislation on the lives of disabled people. Despite legislation, disabled people of working age often face battles within the workplace to ensure that 'reasonable adjustments' (The Equalities Act, 2010) are put in place and maintained:

> A number of the things that she has raised are issues that I thought had already been dealt with through reasonable adjustment like time keeping for example. My recorded start time is 8:15, my hours are 8:15 to 4:15, but I have a reasonable

> adjustment so that I can arrive up to 8:30 as long as I then work till 4:30. My manager was questioning whether I actually stick around until 4:30 because her own working arrangements mean that she's not there between 4:00 and 4:30 to physically witness it and I got rather naffed off about it so apparently there's going to be another meeting so, I'm joining a union!
>
> (Interviewee 2)

When Interviewee 2 finds herself at risk in her workplace, she is forced to engage with issues of *social justice*. The impact of collective politicisation on disabled people has long been recognised (Oliver, 1990). Yet, this move towards political engagement in 2012 is a direct reflection of increased politicisation in a time of recession. Sadly, these politicised engagements were not always available as a support to disabled people in the study. Interviewee 3 had no support from the union in her workplace:

> When I tried to point out it was a disability related absence and there had to be reasonable adjustments she said 'oh well the adjustments are only reasonable if we think they are and as soon as we think they are unreasonable then we can dismiss you'. I gave her the leaflet explaining what the symptoms were and she didn't even look at it she put it straight into a folder.
>
> (Interviewee 3)

Chris told us that he felt he had earned the right to work flexibly in his workplace, because people knew that he delivered and did his job well, but that the flexibility his current job offered also meant that he would be hesitant about taking a risk and applying for a different job. In this sense the work communities that disabled people feel they are able to participate in are limited by the commitment and flexibility of others.

Bodies (In-The-Workplace)
As we have seen, disabled people in work experience high degrees of uncertainty. However, some of this uncertainty arises when disabled peoples' experiences of work are shaped by the interaction between their bodily impairments and their colleagues' reactions to what is seen as bodily difference. Discussion of the body and the role it plays in relation to disability is hotly contested in disability studies. So, we need to take a moment to make three general observations:

1. The body is not solely a concern for disabled people (e.g. pain or the limits of the body impact upon everyone);
2. The way we feel, experience, sense and live in our bodies is always influenced by wider social and community relationships;
3. All of us, if we are not already impaired, can be described as being 'TAB': temporarily abled bodied (Marks, 1999) so, in this sense, all bodies are precarious entities.

(Runswick-Cole & Goodley, 2012)

Disabled people, in the study, feared that some time in the future their impairment, or the failure of others to accommodate their bodies or impairment, would mean that they might no longer be able to work:

> I know I've been ill in the past, so I've got to have that contingency [savings] there. We are moving into a new building shortly and I've got real worries about access issues. Technically because of my spina bifida, I'm doubly incontinent but I manage it to the point where I rarely have accidents but I need to be able to get to the toilet very quickly. Fortunately both my managers are female so I've been able to

> be quite open about it. I've been in this job eight years and they've been aware of this. But now I face being in an office where I have to get through about five heavy fire doors and travel about thirty metres to the nearest toilet, which is going to be outside the door to a lecture theatre that holds about two hundred and fifty students, and it's the only toilet accessible from our office. The writing's on the wall. I know that that toilet is going to be abused, I know that that toilet is going to be full when I need to use it.
>
> (Interviewee 2, disabled person)

Relationships

We have argued that resilience emerges, not within the bodies and minds of isolated individuals, but in relationships between people and in access to resources. In the workplace, disabled peoples' *bodies* were constructed by and experienced through *relationships* with colleagues. This clearly had a big impact on how people experienced work that impacted on their sense of resilience:

> It was very difficult getting back to work as well because people's understandings and perceptions are very tricky to deal with. It took people a year to realise that there was a genuine problem. ... I think people find that hard to understand when they see that you suffer from muscle aches or whatever they think: "oh, just have a hot bath and you will be alright", but it doesn't work like that. I think because on the good days I can do loads, then they can't understand there might be another day when I can't get anything done.
>
> (Interviewee 3)

These *relationships* were particularly troubled by the absence of a 'visibly different' *body*. This caused difficulties for disabled people who were not seen to conform to stereotypical norms of what their colleagues felt a disabled person should look like (see also Dalgin & Bellini, 2008):

> There is just this overall perception that people with depression are supposed to be some cowering wreck in the corner crying and that I am not. Or they have this kind of stigma attached to a mental health condition and they don't see me as a lunatic, coming out of an asylum or something. They have this vision of what a person with clinical depression should be and I don't fit it. So when I tell them they say "really?!"
>
> (Interviewee 4)

'Cripping' the Norms

The stories above reveal the complex interconnections between work and other resources such as relationships, identity, social justice, communities and bodies in terms of building (or indeed draining) resilience. We have tried to show how these accounts unsettle traditional understandings of resilience and disability. However, so far, the notion of work in these accounts has remained undisturbed. So here we consider how disabled people have 'cripped' (McRuer, 2006), or unsettled, normative notions of work and to do that we begin with a story collected as part of the project:

> Neil has the label of Profound and Multiple Learning Disabilities. His parents were told that they should leave him in an institution because he would 'destroy their marriage'. His mother, who was six months pregnant at the time, was offered a termination so that she did not bring another child 'like that' into the world. Neil is 28, he lives in his own home with support from carers and he has a job. For one hour each day, he takes the post from a local business to the post office. He has just learnt to carry the parcels by himself.
>
> (Researcher's notes)

We would argue that Neil is a resilient young man. Neil has bounced back, not by succeeding in spite of the presence of impairment, but by overcoming the devastatingly negative expectations of the professionals who diagnosed him. Neil is not a striving, able individual, meeting developmental norms despite his impairment, rather his resilience is built in relationships with others, particularly his parents, and they have together created a network of resources which enable Neil to work. Neil works one hour a day and this hour has enabled him to feel part of the local community, to build relationships with colleagues, to have a sense of himself as a worker, to have some power and control in his life. We would argue that for Neil work is also a political act, in which he invokes social justice for himself and his family and other disabled people.

In our attempts to 'crip the norms' of work we draw on another story:

> I've found it very hard to recruit people. I've used a [website] but ... I've also tended to employ people who haven't worked in social care for that long and are not set in their ways, so I can train them a bit myself.
>
> (Interviewee 5)

Sarah is an employee *and* an employer. At a time of economic downturn, when disabled people are being characterised as benefit scroungers, the focus has been on what disabled people *take from* the economy; sadly little attention has been paid to the contribution that disabled people *make to* the economy. In 1992, Albrecht identified the stakeholder groups in the political economy of disability and rehabilitation. These, of course, included disabled people but Albrecht also identified health care professionals, hospitals, therapy businesses, home care agencies, assisted living facilities, pharmaceutical companies, technological businesses, banks, lawyers and accountants specialising in disability as well as government and lobby groups. If we add disabled children, this list would also include a raft of 'special education' professionals (Mallett & Runswick-Cole, 2012). The profits of the disability business are huge but, of course, it is not disabled people who benefit from them – directly or indirectly, it seems. Despite the contribution disabled people make, they are still most likely to be portrayed as a drain on the economy in the press.

Conclusions
In this chapter, we have set out to explore the interconnections between disability, work and resilience in the context of economic downturn. In doing so we have sought to trouble traditional approaches to disability, work and resilience. First, by paying attention to the social production of resilience and disability, and then by trying to 'crip' the norms in relation to the world of work. We end with a note of caution: work is not a panacea in relation to the building of resilience in the lives of disabled people; paid work outside the home may not be possible or desirable for all and, yet, as Neil's story reveals, it is possible to re-think the relationships between disability, resilience and work in ways that promote the inter-connections.

Acknowledgements
The authors would like to thank Scope for commissioning the project and for being a critical friend. We would like to thank all the participants in the project for sharing their time and their expertise.

References

Albrecht, G. L. (1992). *The disability business: Rehabilitation in America.* London, United Kingdom: Sage.

Barnes, C. (2008). Generating change: Disability culture and art. *Behinderung und Dritte Welt (Journal for Disability and International Development), 19*(1), 4–13.

Boyden, J. (2001). Childhood and the policy makers: Comparative perspective on the globalization of childhood. In A. James & A. Prout. *Constructing and reconstructing childhood* (pp. 187–211). London, United Kingdom: Routledge.

British Medical Association (BMA) (2012). *Scrap work capability assessment doctors demand.* Retrieved from http://bma.org.uk/news-views-analysis/news/2012/june/scrap-work-capability-assessment-doctors-demand

Butler, P. (2012, July 10). Government confirms closure of factories employing disabled people. *The Guardian.* Retrieved from http://www.guardian.co.uk

Children's Society (2011). *Four in every 10 disabled children living in poverty.* Retrieved from http://www.childrenssociety.org.uk/news-views/press-release/four-ten-disabled-children-are-living-poverty

Contact a Family (2014). Childcare affordability trap. Retrieved from http://www. cafamily.org.uk/media/773401/childcare_affordability_trap_research_june_2014.pdf

Daily Mail. (2011). BMWs for thousands as friends and relatives of the disabled use luxury 'Motability' cars. *Daily Mail.* Retrieved from http://www.dailymail.co.uk

Dalgin, R., & Bellini, J. (2008). Invisible disability disclosure in employment interview: Impact on employers' hiring decisions and views of employability. *Rehabilitation Council Bulletin, 40*(1), 31–44.

Department for Work and Pensions (DWP). (n.d.). *Access to work*. Retrieved from https://www.gov.uk/access-to-work/overview

Department for Work and Pensions. (2010). *Work choice*. Retrieved from https://www.gov.uk/work-choice/overview

Disability Alliance. (2011). *Incapacity benefits migration*. Retrieved from http://www.disabilityalliance.org/ibmigrate.htm

Goggin, G., & Newell, C. (2004). Fame and disability: Christopher Reeve, super crips and infamous celebrity. *M/C Journal, 7*(5), 48–78.

Grant, E. (2011). *The future of the PIP – A social model based approach*. Retrieved from http://www.scope.org.uk/campaigns/publications/future-pip

HMSO. (2010). *The Equalities Act*. London, United Kingdom: Her Majesty's Stationery Office.

Inclusion London. (2011). *Bad news for disabled people: How newspapers are reporting disability*. Retrieved from http://www.inclusionlondon.co.uk.

Lave, J., & Wenger, E. (1991). *Situated learning: Legitimate peripheral participation*. Cambridge, United Kingdom: Cambridge University Press.

Mallett, R., & Runswick-Cole, K. (2012). Commodifying autism: The cultural contexts of 'disability' in the Academy. In D. Goodley, B. Hughes, & L. J. Davis (Eds.), *Disability and social theory* (pp. 33–51). Basingstoke, United Kingdom: Palgrave Macmillan.

Marks, D. (1999). *Disability: Controversial debates and psychosocial perspectives*. London, United Kingdom: Routledge.

Masten, A. S. (2001). Ordinary magic: Resilience processes in development. *American Psychologist, 56*(3), 227–238.

McRuer, R. (2006). *Crip theory: Cultural signs of queerness and disability*. New York, NY: New York University Press.

Office for Disability Issues. (2011). *Disability facts and figures: An overview of UK disability statistics from the Office of Disability Issues.* Retrieved from http://www.nidirect.gov.uk/the-office-for-disability-issues

Oliver, M. (1990). *The politics of disablement*. Basingstoke, United Kingdom: Macmillan.

Oliver, M. (2004). If I had a hammer: The social model in action. In J. Swain, S. French, C. Barnes, & C. Thomas (Eds.), *Disabling barriers, enabling environments* (2nd ed., pp. 7–12). London, United Kingdom: Sage.

Roulstone, A. (2011). *Coalition disability policy – A consolidation of neo-liberalism or benign pragmatism?* Retrieved from http://www.social-policy.org.uk/lincoln2011/Roulstone%20P4.pdf.

Runswick-Cole, K., & Goodley, D. (2012). *Resilience in the lives of disabled people across the life course: A literature review.* Retrieved from http://disability-resilience.posterous.com/pages/findings.

Runswick-Cole, K., & Goodley, D. (2013). Resilience: A disability studies and community psychology approach. *Social and Personality Psychology Compass, 7*(2), 67–78.

Swain, J., & French, S. (2000). Towards an affirmation model of disability. *Disability & Society, 15*(4), 569–582.

Ungar, M. A. (2004). Constructionist discourse on resilience: Multiple contexts, multiple realities among at-risk children and youth. *Youth & Society, 35*(3), 341–365.

Ungar, M. (2005). Introduction: Resilience across cultures and contexts. In M. Ungar (Ed.), *Handbook for working with children and youth: Pathways to resilience across cultures and contexts* (pp. xv–xxxix). Thousand Oaks, CA: Sage.

Ungar, M. (2007). Contextual and cultural aspects of resilience in child welfare settings. In I. Brown, F. Chaze, D. Fuchs, J. Lafrance, S. McKay, & S. Thomas-Prokop (Eds.), *Putting a human face on child welfare* (pp. 1–24). Toronto, Canada: Centre of Excellence for Child Welfare.

Young, A., Green, E., & Rogers, K. (2008). Resilience and deaf children: a literature review. *Deafness Education International, 10*(1), 40–55.

CHAPTER 8

COMPLEXITY, CAPACITY AND CAMBODIA: THE NEOLIBERALISATION OF SPACE AND SCALE

Jonathon Louth

This chapter focuses on how the political economy of international, regional, national and local spaces is imagined and (re)produced through a language of scientific metaphors derived from Newtonian thought that underscores a capitalist logic of expansionism. In particular, it looks at the integration of Cambodia into a wider regional economy and the manner in which this process is shaped by institutions, such as the Asian Development Bank (ADB) and the International Monetary Fund (IMF), which embody an expansionary capitalist logic disguised in seemingly 'natural' Newtonian concepts of space. In respect to this volume on work, the chapter offers an example as to how both macro-level 'drivers' and the meta-theoretical implication of the constant (re)production of particular discursive acts sustain the "repressive confines" of everyday agency in which work takes place (Hobson & Seabrooke, 2006, p. 15). The first part of the chapter develops a position that both space and order are socially produced. It is suggested that the *perceived space* and the assumed *naturalness* of order govern day-to-day activities. Moreover, as the assumptions of the space 'we are in' replicates and reproduces across multiple scales, the worlds of work and society are shaped and bounded accordingly. The chapter argues that the perceived *capacity* to act is constrained by the parameters established via the acceptance of such socially produced spaces. Overall, this line of enquiry locates the argument at the meta-theoretical level, where the intellectual baggage of Western scientific thought, in particular the adherence to a Newtonian paradigm, abstracts order and space as absolute and independent concepts. The second half of the chapter illustrates – via a brief example of the current Cambodian experience of integration into the wider regional economy – that such discursive practices inform the advice of institutions that are central to the governance of the global economy. The consequence is that regional and international financial institutions determine what they consider to be the best course of action within a reified and abstracted notion of what is deemed possible based on an appropriation of Newtonian concepts of space. Moreover, this notion of *capacity* represents a neoliberal framing of space that is radically changing the worlds of work and society. Certainly the focus in this chapter is on Southeast Asia, but it is representative of a multi-scaler process that is reproduced in novel ways across multiple sites on a global and multi-dimensional scale. To illuminate this messy state of affairs, the chapter absorbs a complexity thinking perspective (see Louth, forthcoming), giving cautious consideration to its recognition of emergent, feedback-driven and co-constituting processes. Complexity thinking reveals how reductionist and linear thought continues to drive conventional and accepted responses to the appropriate oversight of economies, regional integration arguments and, ultimately, how everyday people access (and are constrained) by the world of 'work'. Indeed, work can then be understood as an activity that is defined by the (neoliberal) assumptions inherent within broader macro-economic imperatives, yet is sustained by micro-economic compliance and acceptance.

It is 'within' this space that neoliberalism as an ideology can be better understood. It is not about grasping for a caricature on which to attach a straw man argument, instead it is about revealing the ontological presuppositions that define neoliberalism's scope and reveal its manifold reproduction. As an economic approach, neoliberalism's beginnings can be traced to Austrian School teachings of the 1940s (especially the work of Friedrich von Hayek), which drew on the 'scientific', 'pure' and Newtonian mathematical teachings of neoclassical economics (and, of course, the classical teachings of Adam Smith). However, it wasn't until the economic crises (rising energy costs, stagflation, etc.) of the 1970s that neoliberalism as it is now known took recognisable shape. Putting it in crude terms, the project of embedded liberalism that followed the 1944 formation of the Bretton Woods institutions (IMF, World Bank, etc.), accompanied by Keynesian (demand-side) approaches that had risen to prominence in response to the Great Depression of the 1930s, was challenged by the monetarist (supply-side) policies of the emerging neoliberals. Among advanced Western economies it was the governments of Margaret Thatcher in the UK and Ronald Reagan in the US that embodied this shift. The monetarist policies, reflecting the work of Milton Friedman (a formative member of the Chicago School) whose deregulatory position towards market orientated solutions far exceeded those of his friend Hayek, focused on a minimal state (beyond regulatory, institutional and structural functions: supply of money; legal framework; police; defence, etc.), with an emphasis on the rolling back of welfare provision and state involvement in industry and associated services. Within this economic space the supposed free market principles of neoliberalism were espoused as a *natural* unencumbered freedom. This includes policies of privatisation (e.g. of state owned enterprises), deregulation (e.g. of the labour market) and outsourcing (e.g. of social service provision), while lionising the atomised and rational individual (that is, the consumer or entrepreneur) (Harvey,

2005). Yet despite there being a recognisable 'programme', it is worth noting that there is not a universal or a singular notion of what neoliberalism is – its *form* shifts depending on the context. This is why understanding the roots of neoliberalism is so very important. What it takes from economic neoclassicism is not 'accuracy', but merely the (selective) reassurances of a scientific paradigm that parades the 'certainty' of "abstract quasi-mathematical modelling" (Hay, 2004, p. 520). And it is the Chicago School of Friedman that is routinely acknowledged, not just for its well-documented role in the development of neoliberalism, but for its role of celebrating neoclassical economics as a "core scientific theory" (Van Horn & Mirowski, 2009, p. 139).

Thus it can be seen that the dominant discourse is shaped at the meta-theoretical level: (Newtonian) science as universal, science as absolute, science as natural – and then the leap: economics *is* science; economics as promoted via neoliberal orthodoxy is *natural*. Yet neoliberalism is not even a coherent economic theory – it is simply a political ideology that adheres to an often convenient mix of convictions of which certain fundamentals of neoclassical economics form a bedrock (see Brenner & Theodore, 2002). And, despite the inherent contradictions (e.g. persistent poverty, environmental degradation, etc.), it is this outlook that has become the prevailing common sense; it is hegemonic. The space of possibilities – the capacity to act – is constrained to align with this orthodox position. This has become the dominant discursive space within which the international political economy – at multiple scales (international, national, local) – is reproduced. This has meant the (re)creation or the (re)alignment of international institutions and global governance frameworks to reflect this new(ish) orthodoxy. The remainder of this chapter explores how this abstract space of science and economics is a form of domination, despite the limitations of Newtonian science. The work of Henri Lefebvre plays an important role, coupled with insights from complexity thinking, to expose the domination and to reveal its persistence irrespective of contradictions. Then the chapter turns to how this resilient and expansionary hegemonic logic has begun the process of absorbing a small post-conflict Southeast Asian country into this brave, new wider political economy. Of course, as there is now a 'pure' form of neoliberalism it occurs with Cambodian characteristics. It is within this repressive space that Cambodian society and work is being reshaped.

Spatial Awareness
Isaac Newton stated that he could "calculate the motion of heavenly bodies but not the madness of people" (Suzuki, 2007, pp. 173–174). This was his response to the bursting of the South Sea bubble in 1720. Newton had invested heavily in the rising stock price of the South Sea Company, but by year's end he had lost in excess of £20,000 (Suzuki, 2007). People, it would seem, do not behave as heavenly bodies; the movement (and reactions) of social entities are not so easily predicted. Unfortunately this experience did not dissuade the reification of Newton's work beyond the physical sciences. Despite Newton's own personal financial difficulties, the absorption of the Newtonian paradigm, very much in the Kuhnian sense, continued unabated (Louth, 2011).[1] His work, represented by

---

[1] Of course, as the philosopher of science Thomas Kuhn noted, the problem with paradigms is that irregularities that emerge within a dominant and established way of understanding or approaching (scientific) knowledge are usually either ignored or *made* to fit within the established order (Kuhn, 1962).

his laws of motion and gravity, fixed the way in which the world was thought to function. Yet, Newton's work did not simply reconfigure the *scientific* imagination: seemingly, the Western imagination had become bound and restricted by an abstracted and objective truth. Newtonianism, then, reflects the transcendence of Newton's work from a method of scientific enquiry, to that of a series of meta-theoretical presuppositions that captured and bound the social imagination. Space is "produced" in accordance with such Newtonian assumptions (see Urry, 2001, pp. 9–11).

The idea that space is produced and not 'natural' does not necessarily come easily. Henri Lefebvre recognised the peculiarity of the claim, noting that it is a consequence of the general acceptance that space is something we just fill up; that it exists independently of us (Lefebvre, 1991). The absorption of Newtonian thought – along with Cartesian and Euclidian influences – beginning in the seventeenth century and reaching its zenith in the nineteenth century, produced an 'objective' and 'scientific' space. It is most commonly thought of as a "dimension in which matter is located" or conceptualised as "a grid in which substantive items are contained" (Agnew, 2011, pp. 316-317). The "substantive items" (Agnew, 2011, pp. 316-317) incorporate and subsume 'place', constituting place as having a mere geometric and locatable dimensionality (Harvey, 2006). Lefebvre (1976) overturned these notions, arguing that space "has always been political and strategic" and that it is "filled with ideologies" (pp. 30-31). Moreover, he recognised that scientific method and procedure infiltrates mental space, which, in turn, comes to represent social space. This, Lefebvre quickly points out, becomes the "veil of ideology" (1991, p. 106). This idea resonates with Robert Cox's (1981) maxim that "theory is always for someone and for some purpose", the notion that every perspective is a product of its "position in time and space" (p. 128). How then is it produced? How does it find its position within this space? Complexity theory would focus on points of attraction and patterned behaviour – what are termed strange attractors, [2] but Lefebvre (1991) created a conceptual triad to justify his claim that "*(Social) space is a (social) product*" (p. 26). The dialectical triad consists of: "spatial practice"; "representations of space"; and "representational space": put simply it is the perceived world, the conceived world, and the lived world (Lefebvre, 1991, pp. 33, 40).

What Lefebvre captured with his three spatial realms are points of separation between domination, imagination and the day-to-day. It is, however, a little too neat and taxonomically convenient. He offers a lovely metaphor to explain how space can be differentiated in such a manner: "[t]he 'heart' as *lived* is strangely different from the heart as thought and perceived" (Lefebvre, [1974] 1991, p. 40). This is a step away from Cartesian dualism, the heart is divided into three, but each field of space is conceived to exist as a foundational and unavoidably reductionist starting point. There is a dialectic

---

[2] For a 'complexity' understanding this relates to the concept of 'strange attractors'. A strange attractor is the boxing in of far-from-equilibrium systems within what is often called phase or state space. It is the production and reproduction of points of attraction within a feedback-driven non-linear system while still allowing bounded and historically contingent novelty. Systems can be stable for long periods of time, but can exhibit rapid and unpredictable change. (Kauffman, 1993). Such systems are characterised by self-organisation and emergence meaning that should an element fail, decompose or simply be removed, then systems can reorganise, making compensations which may or may not result in changes or niches to the overall system (Eidelson, 1997).

present, each sphere influencing the other, but emergent practices are not sufficiently explored in most descriptions of Lefebvrian space. The triumph of capitalist space is taken as a *fait accompli*, or reads as an argument that has been reverse engineered, neatly explaining the order of things. Yet, Lefebvre, while acknowledging the need to reduce, was deeply opposed to scientific reductionism (Lefebvre, [1974] 1991). Incorporating lessons from complexity thinking allows for a re-invigoration of his ideas. Within his description of dialectical composition of social space there is an acknowledged "dynamism ... to *all* matter and reality" (Merrifield, 1993, p. 517). What should be incorporated into this description is that this is a *high energy* affair. The production of social *spaces* is the result of emergent phenomena that arise through dynamic interactions, the production of which should not be thought of as an entropic or equilibrium-seeking process. The concept of emergence embraces the historicism of Lefebvre (and Marx), but speaks to the novelty of how the "regularities of behavior" within a given system (or ensemble of systems (Kauffman, 1993, p. 210) can be said to transcend its (or their) composite parts (Kavalski, 2007, p. 439). How we understand the interaction of 'parts' relates to what we consider to be the parts (and what we consider the boundary conditions to be). This impacts how we view the international political economy, the theories we use to explain it, and the reified objects within it that we deem to be significant.

However, adding a complexity reading to the production of space supports the notion that despite there being territorial constants the reformulation of space continues; whether, for example, in reference to distance, nations or mobilities (Agnew, 2011; see also Urry, 2005). David Harvey's (2003) focus on the tension between "fixity and motion" (p. 101), the recognition of the tension between territorial configuration and the deterritorialisation tendencies of capital, aligns with a complexity reading of non-linear feedback and self-organising co-constituting elements (Brenner, 1998). Unpredictability and novel emergence is intrinsic to complex systems, they are also resilient, can absorb shocks and maintain a perceived level of regularity allowing for the recognition of patterns (the strange attractor). This is consistent with Harvey's claim as to what constitutes a region: basically, capitalist production, inclusive of patterns of capital accumulation, produce "relatively stable configurations" which can be identified as "regions" or "regional *spaces*" (Harvey, 2003, p. 101). By this he means "regional economies that achieve a certain degree of structured coherence to production, distribution, exchange and consumption" (Harvey, 2003, p. 102) within which there is a breadth of scale that incorporates "the totality of productive forces and social relations" (Harvey, 2001, pp. 328–329). It is an example of the *emergent* production of capitalist space that represents a complex assemblage of intersecting systems (see DeLanda, 2006), in which the state (or some other 'substantive item') can be recast as a resilient and adaptive system that co-evolves as part of an assemblage of "intersocietal systems" (Stewart, 2003, p. 333). Neoliberal regionalism, then, is part of the multiscaler production of "new institutional and regulatory landscapes with their own functional logics and imperatives" (Macartney & Shields, 2011, p. 39). It must be stressed, however, that although there may be significant points of dominance, it is non-hierarchical as the interplay between the micro and the macro is co-constitutive, with the whole process "at once torn apart and squeezed together" (Lefebvre, 1991, pp. 365–366). Any discussion of work and society are immediately subsumed by such dynamics and the simultaneity of being torn apart and squeezed back together, indeed, neoliberal expansion relies on such scaled and creative destructions to reproduce a level of self-similarity as a part of its expansionary logic. In the Cambodian contexts this takes into consideration the (often violent) neoliberal re-ordering within its society (see Springer, 2009).

The 'Capacity' Within: The Case of Cambodia
The *Wall Street Journal* recently referred to the opening of the Cambodian Securities Exchange as "a symbol of Southeast Asia's emergence on global stage [sic]" (Hookway & Bellman, 2012). The "global stage" is a reference, inadvertent or not, to the effective integration of Cambodia into the productive capacity and financialisation of capitalist expansion. This is an explanation with pedigree: take, as a starting point, the Bretton Woods era, which embodies the setting-up of the American-led rules of the game, the idea being to create favourable trade conditions for capitalist states. The second stage of this global expansionary logic is the neoliberal period beginning in the 1970s and epitomised by the privatisation and deregulation of national economies. Moreover, it was a processes that was exported 'under the rules of the game' – most notably under the Washington consensus of the late 1980s: a set of fiscal guidelines often attached to financial assistance for (primarily) developing states via institutions like the World Bank or the IMF (Beeson, 2007). Further, it is a process that is being reproduced via an increasing array of institutional arrangements from the Association of Southeast Asian Nations (ASEAN) through to the G20 (Cammack, 2012). This is a fairly orthodox reading of the current state of affairs. Post-conflict Cambodia is simply being absorbed and integrated into the widening global market. It is a "frontier market" (Chiou, 2012) that provides "cheap labor and strategic geographic location" (Murray, 2012, p. 80), and it has become attractive because of

the absence of capital controls, with foreign companies permitted to own 100% of enterprises within the country (Chiou, 2012; Murray, 2012). The orthodoxy, however, belies a Newtonian underpinning that shapes the realms of possibility. Society and, consequently, the lives of workers are (re)produced in accordance with the assumptions of what is deemed both possible and desirable. This limiting of emancipatory potential was evidenced by fieldwork conducted by the author in Phnom Penh.

In December 2009 and March and April 2012, the author conducted semi-structured interviews with a diverse range of International Non-Government Organisations (INGOs) and International Organisations (IOs). The questioning related to perspectives on governance – the idea was to capture the patchwork nature of a contested term, in the process revealing dominant interpretations and discursive descriptions. The interview with the IMF was undertaken at the organisation's well-maintained offices, attached, quite literally, to the National Bank of Cambodia. With that in mind the first question posed to the IMF representative was whether he felt the IMF was "embedded" in the National Bank of Cambodia. To this he replied that he thought the term "embedded" to be "loaded". The IMF, the author was told, considers that its basic role in Cambodia is as an advocate for "macroeconomic and financial stability" and that it is there to simply offer "technical assistance to the central bank"; this is inclusive of "how to develop monetary policy" and appropriate reporting and accountancy methods (IMF, Resident Representative, interviewed by author, Phnom Penh, Cambodia, 8 February 2012). The Resident Representative was very quick to point out and stress that their position is to act in "purely an advisory role". He stated that: as "there is no programme ... there are no conditions" and what exists in Cambodia is a "very open dialogue" which was all about "good surveillance" guided by "pleasant interaction". Here, in the offices of one of the foremost Bretton Woods institutions, physically attached to a developing country's national bank, the IMF felt its position not to be embedded, but that its role is to merely offer macroeconomic advice and guidance. Its remit, its place, the author was told, is to help the Cambodian Government improve and "build capacity" (IMF Resident Representative, interviewed by author, Phnom Penh, Cambodia, February 8 2012). The IMF via its cooperative *and* voluntary relationship was attempting to help, in an auxiliary role, the Cambodian government by advising how to best manage its macroeconomic policies in order to improve its competitiveness and general economic well-being.

The answers were wholly consistent with what may be expected from an in-country IMF Resident Representative, but this serves as an example of an imagined 'natural' order. It is not embeddedness, but assistance. This assistance is tied to concepts and language like 'best practice', 'comparative advantage', 'competiveness' and 'capacity building'. The IMF, according to the rules of the game, is helping Cambodia to do the best it can; to be the best economy it can be. Most interestingly, the terms 'capacity' and, specifically, 'capacity building' were raised in every interview undertaken; irrespective of whether it was a labour organisation, an INGO with a focus on humanitarian assistance, through to a major Bretton Woods-type IO. On the surface this may not appear to be a negative, given that it is about achieving the best outcome from a given situation. Its emphasis is on working out the best way of doing things: how to perform or act in certain situations so as to maximise outcomes. However, as has been clearly articulated, the concept of capacity – particularly when applied as an instrumental term – reveals the nature of a *conceived representation of space* that is produced via scientific and technocratic discursive acts. Capacity, conjures the potential and, in many instances, an optimal space. Capacity, then, is about the unrealised, the untapped, or the inefficiently explored or exploited within a socially produced neoliberal space.

Operationalising – attempting to realise the stated capacity – can occur in a variety of ways. Much of this is achieved 'on the ground' through managerialism, notably, in recent times, by "the globalizing trend of new public management" (Un & Hughes, 2011, pp. 170–171). In his encompassing volume on the Cambodian economy, Han Chuon Naron, a Cambodian Secretary of State within the Ministry of Economics and Finance, wrote of the need to ensure the resilience and prosperity of ASEAN through the establishment of the "single market, sounder economic and regional interconnection, and narrowing development gaps" ([2009] 2012, p. 514) which depends on "improving the capacity for the regulation and supervision of financial markets" ([2009] 2012 p. 520). This capacity is, of course, what Cox refers to as the "machinery of surveillance" (Cox, 1981, p. 145) and it is linked to a neoliberal expansionary logic. Moreover, this mindset is increasingly scaled, as one ADB document reveals, "all the way down" where institutional capacity building is repeatedly linked with monitoring regimes and "deconcentration and decentralization reforms" (Niazi, 2011, pp. 37, 55). Putting it in blunt terms, the regulatory and bureaucratised logic was explained by the author of the report:

> Capacity building is much broader and more difficult than the simple provision of training for councillors and new staff of the subnational administrations. Improved organizational

and institutional structures are required, as are better systems. It is also necessary to address attitudinal and governance issues. Better facilities, more advanced computerized information systems, together with improved scope for service delivery and development of positive attitudes to serve the public are required. (Niazi, 2011, p. 76).

The fondness for the word 'capacity' is significant. In a 61-page glossy ADB report – half of which was taken up with photographs (and the occasional graph) – celebrating 20 years of ADB involvement in Cambodia, the word 'capacity' appears on 37 occasions, and nearly always alongside words like: 'building', 'institutional', 'development', 'community' and 'public financial management' (ADB, 2012). The IMF (2012) in its most recent report prefers to repeat the phrase "supervisory capacity". Indeed, space is a concept continually referred to by the IMF. In the same report it noted a number of key issues, two of which are "fiscal space" and "financial deepening", arguing fiscal space needs to be "rebuilt" and "safeguarded" (IMF, 2012, p. 9). The IMF – in its cooperative capacity – has sought to encourage trade liberalisation, reformed revenue collection, and the development of "new institutional arrangements" to monitor public–private partnerships to allow, in part, for transparent "comparative bidding and dispute resolution mechanisms" (IMF, 2012, pp. 9–10). Financial deepening has been encouraged for a number of factors which include increasing the "supervisory capacity" of the National Bank of Cambodia (IMF, 2012, p. 12), considered especially important for the successful maintenance of the newly launched stock market. These recommendations, keeping in mind that macro-economic advice is closely listened to (IMF Resident Representative, interviewed by author, Phnom Penh, Cambodia, February 8

2012), represent the wider commitment to the integration and optimisation of Cambodian economic space into the wider region and global economic system.

Gravitating Towards Cambodia
The development and implementation of the securities exchange has been a point of interest for a range of institutional bodies, particularly the IMF, ASEAN and the ADB. It is a part of the manifold social production of Cambodia's financial space in accordance with emerging regional governance structures. Spatiality is encapsulated in a 2012 ADB report on deepening ASEAN. The report recognised and promoted a "gravity effect" within emerging financial markets (Gochoco-Bautista & Remolona, 2012, pp. 29–30). The "gravity effect" – an economics *metaphor* – that is modelled and quantified by economists (see Curtis, 2002), is thought to reveal the intensity of trade, particularly when looking at trade liberalisation regimes. Expectations of intensity – whether lower or higher – are explained in *relation* to the effect (Curtis, 2002), with "cross border equity flows" being thought to occur in the same manner as goods transactions, with distance acting as a "proxy for information costs" (Gochoco-Bautista & Remolona, 2012, p. 30). This sits comfortably with IMF (2012) arguments that Cambodia's geographic closeness "to the world's fastest growing markets, and economic rebalancing in Asia" will inform its integration "into the Asian supply chain" (p. 15). Home biases are seen to exist, and are *explicitly* explained by the gravitational pull argument. The ADB identifies other points of gravitational attraction – bank lending, for instance (Gochoco-Bautista & Remolona, 2012) – but a gravity effect could not be a more Newtonian reference point: it can be visualised as an orrery (a mechanised model of the solar system) in which the sun, planets and moons can be

spaced according to their 'mass' and then put into motion according to the conditions found in a precise and absolute Newtonian space. As an 'effect' the ADB does not let up on the analogy, referring to "frictionless trade", tying in to notions of equilibrium and mass (mass being volume of trade) (Deardorff, 1998, p. 12). Yet, friction – the messy world of politics – is always and forever inescapable, the "production, realization and distribution of surplus value" will always be located in very real *places* (Merrifield, 1993, pp. 521–522). Despite this, capitalist accumulation in Cambodia, in Southeast Asia and, more broadly, the Indo-Pacific region is increasingly occurring through financialisation (see Roberts, 2010), further abstracting and reinforcing the idea of the frictionless world of capitalist space.

Gravity, in this sense, is a Newtonian analogy that evidences the power of objective and scientific space. Gravity is a universal force of attraction where there is a proportional relationship dependent upon the mass of the objects, with distance playing an inverse proportional role. An attractive analogy that describes not only 'attraction', but it speaks to Newtonian ontological assumptions of order, predictability and mechanistic cause and effect. There is a naturalness to the description of a gravity effect that infers that optimisation can occur; it places an ontological significance as to how interactions are assumed to take place. However, how does one determine mass or distance within the social sciences? How much mass does one attribute to a regional hub? How is the nature of proportionality measured? Or inverse proportionality in relation to distance? The questions are not so much answered as acted upon.

It is worth re-iterating that there is not so much an issue with the actual word 'capacity'; it is not a word that speaks to an inherent evil. In the context of this article (and the material it examines), what the term captures are the conceivable potentialities within socially produced capitalist space. Moreover, it is a Newtonian space that has the subtext that the world economy, when frictionless and fully realised, is akin to a near perpetual motion machine that needs only occasional entrepreneurial energy inputs (and for people to consume what is produced). Yet, this image of the circulatory 'movement' of capital ignores the contradictions with this system, whether it be class struggle or the extraction of surplus value (e.g. Burnham, 2001). It does not accommodate the impact of emergent and dynamic processes, where, to twist Brian Arthur's (1994) concept of increasing returns, capital accumulation can be understood as a form of positive feedback. Or it fails to take on board the increase of "emergent contradictions" (Urry, 2005, p. 241), the by-products and schisms of globalisation and expansionary capitalism. Orthodox economics – whether we speak of classical Smithian economics or the uber-market orientated neoliberal economics that has been gradually escaping a range of regulatory fetters since the 1970s – closely resembles a belief in a Newtonian orrery-type machine. The setting up, for instance, of a securities exchange in Cambodia can be understood as the continued production of space down to smaller and smaller scales, while, at the same time, speaking to a wider regional narrative. The consequence is that the place of work within society in the Cambodian context is undergoing a 'reshaping' and a 'redefining' to comply with an emerging and abstracted neoliberal space. The transition in Cambodia is quite evident because of the rapid change and impact, but it is a process that is being replicated in all manner of novel ways on a global scale and then re-enforced on a local scale.

Complexity, Capacity and Cambodia

Conclusions

The Cambodian example of 'capacity building', with encouragement from international financial institutions, and the opening of its securities exchange provides a forceful reminder as to how space is *conceived* as an abstract, frictionless concept. Indeed, it has clearly been shown how *representations of space* dominate the *spatial practices* of the day-to-day, with space in Southeast Asia in the process of being (re)produced according to neoliberal principles. The opening of the stock market was greeted with excitement, but it also invited additional regional pressures; both of those factors are reordering and realigning the lives of Khmer people (even if only in an incremental and limited fashion). Cambodian space and the greater Indo-Pacific region will continue to be reshaped and the political economy of the everyday will inform this process. Large institutions and state interest will obviously push much of the change, but a complex dialogic will mean that relational and multi-scaler effects will allow for emergent behaviour and unexpected 'deviations'. Finally, add to all of this a complex dimensionality, and the production of Cambodian 'capacity' has a simultaneity in as much as while Cambodian space is being re-imagined, so too is the wider region and the global political economy. The world of work and everyday lives is bound, restricted, repressed and resisted within this complex and abstracted socially produced space. However, what might be more visible in the rapidly changing Cambodian example (with the current experience mirroring a stage of primitive accumulation), the reshaping of everyday lives in accordance with neoliberal spatial practices is occurring in a diversity of novel ways on a global scale.

References

ADB. (2012). *20 year anniversary 1992–2012. The Asian development bank in Cambodia: from rehabilitation to inclusive growth.* Phnom Penh, Cambodia: Asian Development Bank.

Agnew, J. A. (2011). Space and place. In J. A. Agnew & D. N. Livingstone. *The Sage handbook of geographical knowledge* (pp. 316–330). London, United Kingdom: Sage.

Arthur, W. B. (1994). Positive feedbacks in the economy. *The McKinsey Quarterly, 1*, 81–95.

Beeson, M. (2007). The political economy of security: Geopolitics and capitalist development in the Asia-Pacific. In A. Burke & M. McDonald (Eds.), *Critical security in the Asia-Pacific* (pp. 56–71). Manchester, United Kingdom: Manchester University Press.

Brenner, N. (1998). Global cities, glocal states: Global city formation and state territorial restricting in contemporary Europe. *Review of International Political Economy, 5*(1), 1–37.

Brenner, N., & Theodore, N. (2002). Cities and geographies of "actually existing neoliberalism". *Antipode,* 34(3), 349–379.

Burnham, P. (2001). Marx, international political economy and globalisation. *Capital & Class, 25,* 103–112.

Cammack, P. (2012). The G20, the crisis, and the rise of global developmental liberalism. *Third World Quarterly, 33*(1), 1–16.

Chiou, P. (2012, May 11). Challenges of new Cambodia stock exchange. *CNN.* Retrieved from http://edition.cnn.com/2012/05/10/business/cambodia-stock-exchange/index.html

Cox, R. W. (1981). Social forces, states and world orders: Beyond international relations theory. *Millennium – Journal of International Studies, 10*(2), 126–155.

Curtis, J. (2002). *Multilateralism in a regionalizing world: NAFTA, FTAA, APEC and all that.* Paper presented to Developing Patterns of Regional Trading Arrangements in the Asia-Pacific Region: Issues and Implications workshop, Vancouver, November 11–12.

Deardorff, A. V. (1998). Determinants of bilateral trade: Does gravity work in a neoclassical world? In J. A. Frankel (Ed.), *The regionalization of the world economy* (pp. 7–22). Chicago, IL: University of Chicago.

DeLanda, M. (2006). *A new philosophy of society: Assemblage theory and social complexity.* New York, NY: Continuum.

Eidelson, R. J. (1997). Complex adaptive systems in the behavioral and social sciences. *Review of General Psychology, 1*(1), 42–71.

Gochoco-Bautista, M. S., & Remolona, E. M. (2012). *Going regional: How to deepen Asean's financial markets: ADB Economics working paper series no. 300.* Manila, Philippines: Asian Development Bank.

Harvey, D. (2001). *Spaces of capital: Toward a critical geography.* New York, NY: Routledge.

Harvey, D. (2003). *The new imperialism.* Oxford, United Kingdom: Oxford University Press.

Harvey, D. (2005). *A brief history of neoliberalism.* Oxford, United Kingdom: Oxford University Press.

Harvey, D. (2006). *Spaces of global capitalism: Towards a theory of uneven development.* London, United Kingdom: Verso.

Hay, C. (2004). The normalizing role of rationalist assumptions in the institutional embedding of neoliberalism. *Economy and Society, 33*(4), pp. 500–527.

Hobson, J. M., & Seabrooke, L. (2006). *The case for an everyday international political economy: Working paper no. 26.* Copenhagen, Denmark: International Center for Business and Politics, Copenhagen Business School.

Hookway, J., & Bellman, E. (2012, April 18). Cambodia Joins Stocks Party. *Wall Street Journal*. Retrieved from http://online.wsj.com/article/SB10001424052702304331204577351551608365784.html#articleTabs%3Darticle

IMF Resident Representative. (2012). Interviewed by the Author. Recorded semi-structured interview. IMF Office, National Bank of Cambodia, Phnom Penh, Cambodia, February 8, 2012.

IMF. (2012). *Cambodia 2011 Article IV consultation: IMF Country Report no. 12/46*. Washington, DC: International Monetary Fund.

Kauffman, S. A. (1993). *The origins of order: Self-organization and selection in evolution*. Oxford, United Kingdom: Oxford University Press.

Kavalski, E. (2007). The fifth debate and the emergence of complex international relations theory: Notes on the application of complexity theory to the study of international life. *Cambridge Review of International Affairs, 20*(3), 435–454.

Kuhn, T. (1962). The structure of scientific revolutions. *International Encyclopaedia of Unified Science, 2*(2). Chicago, IL: University of Chicago Press.

Lefebvre, H. (1976). Reflections on the politics of space. *Antipode, 8*(2), 30–37.

Lefebvre, H. ([1974] 1991). *The production of space* [trans. by D. Nicholson-Smith]. Oxford, United Kingdom: Blackwell Publishing.

Louth, J. (2011). From Newton to Newtonianism: Reductionism and the development of the social sciences. *Emergence: Complexity and Organization, 13*(4), 63–83.

Louth J. (forthcoming) 'Uncertain certainties: Resilience and change in global affairs' in E. Kavalski (Ed.), *World politics at the edge of chaos: Reflections on complexity and global life.* Albany, NY: SUNY Press.

Macartney, H., & Shields, S. (2011). Space, the last frontier? A scaler relational approach to critical IPE. In S. Shields, I. Bruff, & H. Macartney (Eds.), *Critical international political economy: Dialogue, debate and dissensus* (pp. 27–42). Basingstoke, United Kingdom: Palgrave Macmillan.

Merrifield, A. (1993). Place and space: A Lefebvrian reconciliation. *Transactions of the Institute of British Geographers, 18*(4), 516–531.

Murray, L. R. (2012). Target Cambodia. *World Policy Journal, 29*, 79–87.

Naron, H. C. ([2009] 2012). *Cambodian economy: Charting the course of a brighter future – A survey of progress, problems and prospects.* Pasir Panjang, Singapore: Institute of Southeast Asian Studies.

Niazi, N. H. (2011). *Deconcentration and decentralization reforms in Cambodia: Recommendations for an institutional framework.* Mandaluyong City, Philippines: Asian Development Bank.

Roberts, J. (2010). The state, empire and imperialism. *Current Sociology, 58*(6), 833–858.

Springer, S. (2009). Violence, democracy, and the neoliberal "order": The contestation of public space in post-transitional Cambodia. *Annals of the Association of American Geographers, 99*(1), 138–162.

Stewart, P. (2003). Complexity theories, social theory, and the questions of complexity. *Philosophy of the Social Sciences, 31*(3), 323–360.

Suzuki, T. (2007). The East Asian development model in the era of global finance: The case of Japan. *Southeast Asian Review of Asian Studies, 29*, 173–191.

Un, K., & Hughes, C. (2011). The political economy of good governance. In C. Hughes & K. Un (Eds.), *Cambodia's Economic Transformation* (pp. 199–218). Copenhagen, Denmark: Nordic Institute of Asian Studies Press.

Urry, J. (2001). Sociology of space and place. In J. R. Blau (Ed.), *The Blackwell companion to sociology* (pp. 1–16). Malden, United Kingdom: Blackwell Publishing.

Urry, J. (2005). The complexity of the global. *Theory, Culture and Society, 22*(5), 235–254.

Van Horn, R., & Mirowski, P. (2009). The rise of the Chicago School of Economics and the birth of neoliberalism. In P. Mirowski & D. Plehwe (Eds.), *The road from Mont Pelerin: The making of the neoliberal thought collective*. Cambridge, MA: Harvard University Press, pp. 139–180.

INDEX

able-bodiedness 11
affection 13
    empathy 13
    compassion 13, 52
    love 12, 13
Asian Development Bank 196

belonging 149, 167, 176
bingo 97, 99, 113
blame and responsibility 40, 44, 50, 52, 59

Cambodia 205
capacity building 207-208, 212
capitalism 100-101, 114, 212
care 17
    non-professional 17, 18, 21
    rationality of 18
career 74, 76, 80, 96
career criminality 128, 133, 139
choice and free will 74, 77
Christianity 97
citizen-carers 11
citizenship 14
class 11, 90, 96, 147, 148, 212
community cohesion 153, 179
complexity theory 202,
Coroner's verdict 42-43
coronial inquest 42-43
cripping 189-190

democracy 151, 154, 166,
Department of Education 153
dependence-independence dichotomy 29
deregulation of economies 205
disability rights 191

edge work 125
emotion (sociology of) 17
emotional energy 20, 23, 28
emotional stratification 21
empowering 14, 22, 32
enterprise 98, 126
entrepreneurship 95
equality 11, 30, 179
ethics of care 29
ethnicity 11

family 17, 44, 178
feminist/feminism 18, 30
football 102, 111–113
further education 147, 151

gambling 97
gay and lesbian parenthood 24
gender and gambling 98
great depression 198
grief 38, 44, 51

habitual offenders 127
Hague Convention 86
'hard to reach' learners 146
hegemony 154
honour and pride 89

Index

iatrogenic harm 37, 64
impairment 58, 175
incapacity benefit 181
industry 111, 147, 198
inequality 14, 31, 148
International Monetary Fund 196

labour markets 153
late modernity 122
liberalisation regimes 210
loss 39, 51
lottery 103-109

malfeasance 38, 59, 64
masculinity 73
military combat 75
military covenant 88, 90
misfeasance 38, 59, 61, 64

National Anti-Gambling League 109
neoliberalism 151, 197, 199
new penology 123, 139
Northern Atlantic Treaty Organization (NATO) 81
Not in Employment Education or Training (NEET) 147

parenthood 17
pleasure 123
pools 102, 111
poverty and gambling 103
Prince's Trust 147
prison 43, 131
professional mistakes 39

public service workers 38, 60
Pygmalion effect 166

race 12, 148
reciprocal causation 157–158
reciprocity 146
recourse and redress 54
recruitment (military) 73
regional economies 204
religion 12
resilience, 73, 173, 174
risk society thesis, 122
risk-taking, 101, 123, 137

same-sex parenting 25
secondary victimisation 57–58
self-efficacy 146, 157
self-empowerment 14, 23
self-inflicted death 37
self worth 29
sexual orientation 12, 30
social exclusion 30, 147
social justice 11, 149
social policy 31
soldier 73
status and power 19
suicide 43

tertiary victimisation 37, 55
theft 96, 139
transformative learning 146

unconventional harms 37

Index

victimological other 53
victimology 37, 55
voluntary risk 123

Werther Effect 45
work capability assessment 181